Atlanta's Garden Plants

Roy L. Heizer

Photography by Nancy Heizer

4880 Lower Valley Road · Atglen, Pennsylvania 19310

Schiffer Books are available at special discounts for bulk purchases for sales promotions or premiums. Special editions, including personalized covers, corporate imprints, and excerpts can be created in large quantities for special needs. For more information contact the publisher:

Published by Schiffer Publishing Ltd.
4880 Lower Valley Road
Atglen, PA 19310
Phone: (610) 593-1777;
Fax: (610) 593-2002
E-mail: Info@schifferbooks.com

For the largest selection of fine reference books on this and related subjects, please visit our website at:
www.schifferbooks.com
We are always looking for people to write books on new and related subjects. If you have an idea for a book please contact us at the above address.

This book may be purchased from the publisher.
Include $5.00 for shipping.
Please try your bookstore first.
You may write for a free catalog.

In Europe, Schiffer books are distributed by
Bushwood Books
6 Marksbury Ave.
Kew Gardens
Surrey TW9 4JF England
Phone: 44 (0) 20 8392 8585;
Fax: 44 (0) 20 8392 9876
E-mail: info@bushwoodbooks.co.uk
Website: www.bushwoodbooks.co.uk

Designed by RoS
Type set in Adobe Caslon Pro/Souvenir Lt BT

ISBN: 978-0-7643-3810-6
Printed in China

CONTENTS

$\mathcal{A}$CKNOWLEDGMENTS

I'd like to thank my friends and family for their support of this project, and everyone at Schiffer Publishing.

Special thanks goes to the following organizations:

~The Atlanta Botanical Garden
~ The State Botanical Garden of Georgia
~ The Master Gardeners of Atlanta
~ Callaway Gardens
~ Sacred Heart Catholic Church in Augusta, GA
~ The city of Athens, GA
~ The city of Augusta, GA
~ The city of Macon, GA
~ Coastal Wildscapes
~ The North Carolina Nursery and Landscape Assn.
~ The South Carolina Nursery and Landscape Assn.
~ The Georgia Green Industry
~ The Tour of Homes and Gardens
~ The Savannah Book Festival

Author's note: Coastal Wildscapes is a non-profit native plant organization. For more information, please visit Coastalwildscapes.org.

ℐNTRODUCTION

Atlanta holds many wonders for the modern or traditional gardener. With this book, explore the history, folklore, and science of some of America's most wonderful garden and landscape plants. Long summers and relatively mild winters allow gardeners to find flowers blossoming and lush evergreens year round in North Georgia.

Find out which flowering perennial was used for courting, how the Thistle became the national emblem of Scotland, and which garden plants are traditionally included in religious services. Do you know what Saskatoon, Canada, has to do with Atlanta, Georgia? Arranged in alphabetical order by botanical name to be reader friendly with clear color photographs that were all taken in their natural environment using natural light, *Atlanta's Garden Plants* tells the story of the flowers, plants, and trees that can be seen growing in and around Atlanta.

This book may also be used as a plant identification guide, as it takes the reader outside the average gardening experience, to see garden flowers and trees from a wider perspective, all while having the fun that drew gardeners' to plants in the first place. Enjoy visiting the State Botanical Garden of Georgia or North Georgia's many other gardens while learning a new fact or folklore story that can be passed on to your friends.

ABELIA TO ZELKOVA

ATLANTA'S GARDEN PLANTS

ABELIA

Also called: *Heaven's Horn*

Abelia is a medium sized evergreen shrub in the North Georgia landscape. It is covered with small almost heart shaped leaves that can vary in color from glossy green to yellow. Abelias produce an abundance of small bell or trumpet shaped flowers that emerge in spring and last into fall. Their colors range from white to pink and they can be pruned to shape with impunity.

Originally native to China, Abelia is an old fashioned garden shrub and is most often grown for the flowers ability to attract butterflies and moths. They have been grown in the American mid-South since before the modern garden center was introduced.

Abelias are sometimes called Heaven's Horn because of the shape of the flower. The flowers of Heaven's Horn can, according to one legend, be seen in the hairpieces of the angels that blow the horns that sound across Heaven. It is said that the radiance of the angels is reflected in the flowers.

In the Jewish tradition, the Fir has been sacred since it was the tree that was hewn for the ceiling of the Temple of Jerusalem.

Some remains of the Fir's folklore association still lingers in the Hartz. There girls dance about the Fir tree in their religious festivals. While they decorate the tree with lights, flowers, eggs and fruit, they sing songs that are not Christian. In circling about it this way, they prevent the escape of a dryad concealed among the branches. This dryad, or tree elf, must give to them whatever is in his possession or abandon hope of gaining his freedom. This is said to be the origin of the Christmas tree, and the tree elf has grown to be the benevolent St. Nicholas, Santa Claus or Old Nick. Santa is believed by Grimm and other students of folklore to be none other than Odin himself, Christianized almost beyond recognition.

Germans, when they light the tree on Christmas Eve, make sure that it is Fir and not Pine, Spruce, or Hemlock. If any other tree is used, it will show the fate of the celebrator, provided he is brave enough to look at his shadow on the wall by the tree lights. If he appears without a head, that will signify death in the coming year. If a branch is cut off and laid across the foot of the bed, it will keep away any nightmares. A stick of Fir, not quite burned through, fends off lightning and a bunch put over the barn door keeps out evil spirits that want to steal the cattle.

In the area known as the Black Forest, in Bavaria, there is a tradition of gathering the cones of the Fir and painting them silver and using them as ornaments. If one asks how this tradition came about, he might hear the story of the silver Christmas cones. During a Christmas season many a long year ago, a miner in town fell ill and left his wife and children in dire straits for food and fuel. The wife climbed up into the surrounding mountains, intending to pick up Fir cones that she could sell to make one more day's wages with which to feed her family. As she entered the woods, a little old man with a jolly face and a long white beard emerged from the shadows and pointed to a Fir tree that he said would yield the best cones. When the woman turned back to thank him, he was gone. When she reached the tree there was such a downfall of cones that she almost became overwhelmed. The basket was extraordinarily heavy, too; indeed she could barely reach her home with it, and the reason for this was soon evident, for when she emptied the cones upon the table, every cone was made of silver.

The Fir is a large evergreen conifer. It has short needles that are borne in tight whorls around stout branches. They are almost always a deep green on top with a subtle silver hue on the undersides. The cones begin to develop in the spring after the new growth, and emerge a deep rich burgundy color. The cones mature to a dark brown by mid-summer. The Fir is typically not used for residential urban landscapes because of its enormous size; however, given space it will develop into one of the most graceful of trees.

 CACIA

Also called: *Thorn tree or Wattle*

Acacia, a genus of shrubs and trees belonging to the family Fabaceae, was first described in Africa by the Swiss botanist and author Carolus Linnaeus in 1773. The plants tend to be thorny and pod-bearing. The name derives from the Greek for a sharp point, due to the thorns.

Acacias are also known as thorn trees, for their large anti-social thorns, or wattles. There are many types of Acacias; about half are native to Australia, with the remainder native to warm tropical and sub-tropical regions throughout Africa and the Americas.

ACER RUBRUM

Also called: *Maple or Red Maple*

The Red Maple is one of North Georgia's finest hardwood deciduous trees, with a range from Southern Canada to South Florida. The Red Maple is called Red due to its amazing fall color, with a palette from light yellow to deep red. Its brilliant colors and grand size stand out for miles against a hillside forest. The Acer Rubrum is native to the Eastern United States, while other members of the Acer family are native to Central Europe.

Acer Rubrum is a magnificent tree, especially as it ages. With time, a Red

Maple develops bark that is grey to brown and deeply furrowed. A massive trunk holds up stout branches that reach out and up, holding tri-pointed medium green leaves throughout the summer and displaying structural beauty in the winter.

A Moldavian folklore tale from the Old World tells the story of a King's young daughter who fell in love with a shepherd after he charmed her with a Maple wood flute.

This young daughter went into the fields with her two older sisters to gather the first strawberries of the spring season. Their wretched old father thought so much more of his victuals than of his kingdom or his family, that he promised his kingdom to the first daughter who should return to him with a basket full of fruit. When the young daughter's basket was the first one filled, it maddened the two older sisters into a jealous rage. Hence, they killed her and buried her body under a Maple tree. The two older sisters divided the berries between them and returned with the improbable story that an elk had eaten her. The King's sadness was plain for all to see. Sad, too, were the musings of the Shepherd on the hill. Blow as he might, the Maple wood flute made no sound, nor did his lady appear.

On the third day, the Shepherd, passing the Maple tree beneath which his love was buried, noticed a fair new shoot that had sprung up from the ground at the base of the tree. He cut off the shoot and fashioned a new and more ornate flute, which began to sing when he put it to his lips. The new flute did not sing in wordless notes, but in prophetic lyrics. "Play, dearest! Once I was a King's daughter; then I was a Maple shoot; now I am but a wooden flute."

Astonished at this disclosure, the Shepherd rushed to the palace and demanded an audience with the King. The King was amazed, as well he might be, when he put the flute to his own mouth and heard it say: "Play, my father! Once I was a King's daughter; then I was a Maple shoot; now I am but a wooden flute." Wishing to test his senses, he called to the wicked daughters and commanded that they also blow into the instrument. As each did so, it cried: "Play, murderer! Once I was a King's daughter; then I was a Maple shoot; now I am but a wooden flute." Realizing the atrocity that had been committed, the King drove the daughters from the palace and banished them to a remote and desolate island in the Black Sea. The Shepherd went back to his sheep and assuaged his loneliness with the voice of his beloved.

Also called: *Maidenhair Fern*

The Maidenhair Fern, with its delicate structure and slender fronds, was one of the magic plants in Roman mythology. It was thought to be the hair of Venus, goddess of love, beauty and fertility who had risen from the foam of the sea. This belief was based on a fascinating quality of the Maidenhair. When it is placed underwater, it takes on a silvery sheen and when removed from the water it appears to be completely dry. Water will not stick to the fronds of the Maidenhair Fern. In Roman symbolic myth, a potion made from Maidenhair Fern was considered instrumental in producing grace, beauty and love. In France, Maidenhair Fern is to this day still referred to as Cheveux de Venus — hair of Venus.

Maidenhair Fern is a reliable perennial in the Atlanta shade garden. Like all ferns, the Maidenhair does not flower but adds soft delicate foliage to the texture composition of any shady spot. While Maidenhair needs regular watering, it is not a water plant, and needs to be in a well-drained location.

Also called: *Red Buckeye or Scarlet Buckeye*

Aesculus Pavia, or Red Buckeye, is a deciduous flowering shrub. The Red Buckeye is native to the Southeastern United States, found from Illinois to Virginia in the north and from Florida to Texas in the south.

Red Buckeye is a favorite with native plant enthusiasts. It is one of the first plants with tubular flowers to blossom in the spring and is therefore vital for returning Hummingbirds and early Butterflies. In the North Georgia area it should need no supplemental water or fertilizer beyond its first year.

The Red Buckeye is not only admired for its gorgeous red flower spikes, but also for its unique palmate shaped leaves. The leaf shape gives the Aesculus much of its overall texture. This Horse Chestnut relative also has large, easy to germinate Chestnut style seeds. The seeds and young shoots of this fast grower are poisonous if ingested.

It is normal for this plant to drop its leaves by the later parts of summer, so the spring flower show is its most prominent season. The Red Buckeye is not known for its fall color, but as it ages the branch structure is a strong feature. Like the Crepe Myrtle, severe pruning is not recommended. Gardeners say to let the Red Buckeyes full natural form develop on its own.

Native Americans crushed parts of the Red Buckeye and put them in water to stupefy fish, making it easier to capture them. Historians have noted that a crude soap may be derived from the Red Buckeye roots and a dark dye obtained from the wood.

AGAVACEAE

Also called: *Yucca*

Yucca is a member of the Agave family, Agavaceae. Its numerous species are notable for their rosettes of evergreen, tough, sword like leaves. Most varieties have rigid leaves and sharp points, but there are varieties that are have soft leaves. The soft leafed varieties still have sharp points at the tips. Gardeners must use care when planting or maintaining Yuccas as the sharp points can make them dangerous. Yuccas prefer full sun and dry conditions, making them perfect for the sunny dry slopes of eastern central Georgia. The large white bell shaped flowers sit on tall panicles high above the swirl of leaves. Landscapers will often pick Yuccas for their unique structural form, adding a distinct texture to the full sun border.

Yuccas are native to most of the hot, dry parts of the Americas. Historically, in Georgia, the stiff leaved varieties were called "Spanish bayonet" because of their use by the Spaniards as a bayonet replacement on the battlefields.

All Yuccas are pollinated by Yucca moths, a beneficial insect.

AKEBIA QUINATA

Also called: *Five Leafed Akebia or Chocolate Vine*

The Five Leafed Akebia is a fast growing vine that is native to Japan. It is grown in Japanese style gardens for its ornamental appeal. The Akebia is known for its five-leaf arrangement, giving this long, full growing vine a distinct texture. Unlike other ornamental vines, Akebia is a twining vine that does not attach to walls or fences with roots or suction cups. The Akebia needs to wrap around an object in order to support itself. This twining attribute makes the Five Leafed Akebia easy to cut back and contain. Many gardeners also prefer to use the Akebia as a groundcover. The Akebia is well suited to the Atlanta garden, as it does not handle consistently cold winters or long hot summers.

The flower of the Akebia is dark red to brownish in appearance, leading to the common name Chocolate Vine. The flowers emerge in late spring and last well into the summer.

ALLIUM SCHOENOPRASUM

Also called: *Chive or Chives*

Chives are in the same family as Onions, Leeks, Shallots, and Garlic. Chives are native to Eastern Europe and parts of Asia. Since the fifteenth century C.E. Chives have been common in herb gardens throughout Europe. Chives are hardy, drought tolerant perennials that grow in clumps from underground bulbs. The leaves are round and hollow, similar to onions, but smaller in size. Over the summer, in the Atlanta herb garden, Chives produce large round pink to light purple flowers. The flower head resembles that of a small poppy or peony.

Alliums, in America, are most often used for culinary reasons. They are cut right off the plant and need not be cooked to provide flavor and scent. Most often they are diced into "little rings of crispness." Chives are usually used fresh and are a common addition to baked potatoes, cream soups, pot roasts and egg dishes.

Chives have historically been used for medicinal reasons also, and have been thought to improve digestion and reduce high blood pressure. The oil is said to have antibacterial qualities and unlike most herbs, Chives can be frozen to retain freshness.

AMELANCHIER

Also called: *Serviceberry, Juneberry, or Saskatoon*

Serviceberry is a medium sized, usually multi-trunked shrub in the Rose family. According to an old tradition, the flowers appear in early spring "when the Shad run the river." The fruit is a small berry style pome, red or purple to nearly black when they reach maturity in late June. While the pome is sweet and edible, Serviceberries are most widely planted for their fall color. Depending on the variety, Serviceberries can display a fall color pallet that ranges from yellow to orange, red to russet. The fall color can last for as long as three months.

Juneberry is native to all of North America. Modern day native plant enthusiasts plant the Juneberry as not only an ornamental for its spring flowers and fall color, but also as a source of food. The fruit of the Juneberry shrub strongly resembles the Blueberry in size, color, and shape, although the taste is different. Juneberry jam is a favorite of local organic cooks.

The name Saskatoon originated from a Cree Native American Indian name, Missaskwatoomina or 'mis-sask-quah-toomina', for a type of Amelanchier berry. The Canadian city of Saskatoon, Saskatchewan, is named after this plant.

Native American Indians planted Amelanchier less for its ornamental value, but more as an encompassing food source by way of habitat. Juneberries attract and are browsed by deer and rabbits, as well as several types of moths, butterflies, and birds.

A folklore tale from the Native American tradition tells of how the Serviceberry was called "The timekeeper of the seasons." It was said that the seasons were marked by what the Serviceberry was doing. In the spring when crops could be planted, the Serviceberry was in flower. In the summer, when the crops needed water and compost, the Serviceberry was fruiting. In the fall when the crops could be harvested, the Serviceberry was in color. In the winter when the ground was sleeping, so too was the Serviceberry.

$\mathcal{A}$QUILEGIA

Also called: *Columbine, Jester's Hat, or King's Bouquet*

Columbines, native to Europe, are a well-known garden and wildflower throughout most of America. While perfectly suited to the North Georgia area, gardeners from Ohio to as far west as Colorado grow them in their flowerbeds and borders. In fact, Columbine has been the state flower of Colorado since April 4, 1899. Aquilegias have small spring blossoming flowers in a wide array of pastel colors, from white to purple. Columbine is easy to grow, requiring no more than a little broken shade in the afternoon and occasional rainfall. A perennial, Columbines go down for the winter but return each spring to delight the Atlanta area gardener again.

Columbine gets its two common names, Jester's Hat and King's Bouquet, from the old French story that references the shape of the flower. The story goes that a Jester, or royal clown, was failing one day to amuse the King of Bayeux. The King sent the Jester away to be executed. While locked up in a courtyard awaiting execution the Jester put an Aquilegia flower on his head while laughing that he was about to become a cut flower himself, and therefore would be the King's bouquet. Meanwhile the Queen saw the Jester's flower hat and asked that the Jester and the flower be brought to her at once. Upon seeing the beauty of the flower, the amusing way that the Jester wore it and the flowers resemblance to the Jester's own hat, she spared the life of the Jester. The Aquilegia became a most beloved flower across France, second only in importance to the Iris.

ARTEMISIA

Also called: Wormwood, Southernwood, or Young Lads Love

Artemisia has feathery yellow to green or gray to silver leaves. All Wormwood varieties have lacy, delicate and finely lobed leaves. Some varieties are tall and upright while others are low mounds, either way it has aromatic qualities and is thought to be an aphrodisiac.

According to one old English tale Artemisia was known to be a courting symbol. As the tale goes a young man with a Southernwood sprig on his coat lapel walked past the towns giggling girls, sniffing his sprig as he went. When one of the girls turned back toward him he gave her the Southernwood sprig and so they began their first courting stroll. If, according to the tale, the sprig stayed fresh through the winter, they could marry in the spring. However, if the sprig turned dark it was a sign to them that they were not to marry. In this case it stayed fresh, they married and this is where the common name Young Lads Love comes from.

While several species are grown as ornamental garden plants, Artemisia is also planted and grown around doghouses for its ability to repel fleas and moths.

Also called: *Butterfly Weed or Milkweed*

Butterfly Weed is one of Georgia's best native perennials. Native plant enthusiasts sing its praises because of the butterflies that it brings to the Georgia garden. With flower colors ranging from yellow, red and orange to a mix of these, they also add a splash of warmth to the summer border.

Butterfly Weed is a fun plant for children or beginning gardeners. It is a great lesson in the patience needed, and the rewards of, gardening. Any time of the year, simply cut a piece four to six inches long off an established plant and put it in a cup of water. Wait two to four weeks for roots to develop, and then carefully plant the Butterfly Weed outside directly in the garden during warmer weather. Water it a few times to help it along, then sit back and enjoy it for years to come. Ignore the small yellow Aphids on the branch tips; they are a butterfly food source and a natural part of the plant to insect pollination cycle.

Carolus Linnaeus named the genus after Asclepius, the Greek god of healing and medicine. The Milkweed family is known for its medicinal qualities.

ASTER

Also called: *Daisy or Sunflower*

Historically, all garden flowers have had symbolism. The symbolism associated with the Aster is purity, innocence, beauty, patience and simplicity. In the Christian tradition, the Aster is often depicted in garden scenes with the Virgin Mary. Her purity and goodness is reflected in the bright and radiant flowers that surround her. In many Catholic churches, flowers are brought in as an offering to the Virgin Mary. Aster flowers are also used for decoration in many protestant churches.

The name Daisy come from the term 'Day's eye', because several members of the Aster family only open during the day and close at night. Southern gardeners sometimes call Daisies Summer Sun, since it blooms in the summer when the days are long and sunshine is plentiful. In the Pagan tradition, the Aster is venerated as the embodiment of the sun and the summer season. Pagans believe that as long as the Aster is growing, the god of summer reigns supreme. They also believe that as the days get shorter and the god of winter grows more powerful, the god of summer, and therefore the Aster, must relinquish its power. The belief is that the seasons will eventually rotate again, and that the Aster will return with the warmth of the next season.

The Aster family, Asteraceae, is one of the largest of flowering plants. The name 'Asteraceae' is derived from the Greek word for star, referring to the star shaped flower. The family comprises more than fifteen hundred genera and thousands of species. Asters can be found growing all over the world.

Members of the Aster family that have culinary value include Lettuce, Chicory, Globe and Jerusalem Artichokes, Sunflower, and Safflower. Aster flowers and leaves can be used as herbs or herb substitutes. Chamomile, Echinacea, and Calendula are grown commercially for herbal brews and for the floral trade.

ATHYRIUM

Also called: *Fern, Devil's Bidder, or Japanese Painted Fern*

In old England, Athyrium is believed to be the "Fearn" that gave villages such names as Landisfearn, Fernhurst, Farndale, Farnham, Farningham, and Farnsfield. According to an old Roman Catholic folklore tale, the high priests of the old church told stories of Athyrium and the devil. If one did not attend church and confession regularly, the devil would use Athyrium, a Fern that was plentiful in old England, to unlock the door and enter the home of the wayward sinner. The townsfolk began to call this Fern "Devil's Bidder." If, however, one repented and attended church again, the Fern was rendered powerless to bid the devil. The story ends by saying that all Ferns are the haunts of fairies and spirits.

Another tale of Athyrium says it had the ability to loosen the shoes from a horse's foot if it was to walk over it in a meadow. Indeed, one of this Ferns other names is Unshoe-the-horse.

Although much of the Athyrium's lore comes from England, it is actually native to the entire northern hemisphere. In Syria, the invocation of the spirit of this Fern seems to be indicated in the practice of printing the form of the Athyrium on the hand of a lady about to be married. A frond of this Fern, known to the Syrians as Bride's Glove, is laid on the hand, bound into place, and then the ruddy of dye of the Henna tree is washed over the skin. The back of the hand, covered by the frond, is protected, and the form of it remains as long as the stain.

Most American gardeners are familiar with Japanese Painted Fern, an Athyrium cultivar that is native to China, Japan, and Taiwan.

BEGONIA

Begonias are best known as summer color bedding or container plants. They are so popular that many different cultivars have been created, with lush colors ranging from the purest of white to the deepest of red. The gardener can also find colors in shades of soft pink and fresh salmon. The fleshy leaves are quite the attribute, with leaves on newer cultivars being shaped like the wings of angels or the wings of devils.

Begonias have been the inspiration for many gardening articles, pop culture references, and poems. One such poem, as written by nineteenth century poet K. Eisenstadt, tells of the Begonia's beauty as compared to that of a young lady.

Colors in the summer do not compare
The sky, the trees, the flowers of the field
The rainbow, the tapestries all fail to radiate her beauty
She is as lovely... as only the Begonia!

BIGNONIA CAPREOLATA

Also called: *Crossvine*

A robust evergreen vine and a Southeastern native, Bignonia is considered by many gardeners to be the best flowering plant for mailboxes and fences. It needs the support of a sturdy object to hold it upright. Crossvine is slower growing and more manageable than Wisteria, and is therefore more desirable in a landscaped setting.

The Crossvine has many attributes for the Southern gardener to love, not least among them is its winter color. The Crossvine is an evergreen only in the sense that it keeps it leaves all year. The winter leaf color can vary from deep green to bright red, with shades of yellow and plum. It is named Crossvine due to the cross pattern of the leaf petioles, but the Crossvine's huge trumpet shaped flowers are its most sought after feature. The flowers of the Crossvine look similar to its close relative, Campsis Radicans or Trumpet Vine. The blood orange, tangerine or yellow colored flowers come out early in the spring to greet the returning hummingbirds and to attract butterflies.

Many churches that host outside weddings have discovered the Crossvine for permanent arch trellises under which to conduct their ceremonies. Churches like the symbolism of a Cross-vine for Christian weddings and the full season flowering display provides for a budget conscious event.

Bulbine, a distant relative of Aloe, is a reliable perennial in the Atlanta garden. The fleshy leaves form a spiky whirl of green about six inches high, with the yellow to orange flowers floating above the foliage. Bulbine flowers emerge in mid-June and last well into fall. Bulbine does best in full sun with regular watering or light shade and less water. Like most perennials, no variety of Bulbine should be watered in the winter.

$\mathcal{B}$UXUS SEMPERVIRENS

Also called: *Boxwood, English Boxwood, or Box*

Boxwoods have been important in formal English gardens for centuries and in America since colonial times. The first Boxwood plants were introduced to American gardeners in 1652 and have been utilized ever since. Boxwoods are suitable for formal and informal garden use as a hedge, border, screen, and topiary plant. They are greatly valued for their compact evergreen foliage that is highly accepting of shearing, thus adding immensely to their versatility. All Boxwoods have opposite leaf arrangement, not to be confused with the similar looking Yaupon Holly that has alternate leaf arrangement.

The botanical name Buxus comes from the Latin word for box. This is why, in most of Europe, the Boxwood is known simply as Box. The word Sempervirens also comes from Latin. Semper means always and virens means green; Sempervirens is the Latin for evergreen.

The Boxwood grain is fine, strong and resists splitting. It has historically been used to make jewelry boxes, heirloom chests and personal items such as hair combs. Because of the relatively high density of the wood, Boxwood is often used for Chess pieces. Wooden chess sets almost always use Boxwood for the white pieces and commonly use stained Boxwood for the black pieces, in lieu of ebony. Boxwood is also used for high quality violin and viola fittings, such as pegs and tailpieces. The extremely fine grain of Boxwood makes it suitable for woodblock printing. The earliest known examples of Boxwood woodblocks date to China in the ninth century C.E.

CALADIUM

It is easy to see why this very tender perennial would have a strong presence in the Christian tradition. The leaves of the Caladium certainly do have the shape of Angels' wings as well as the shape of a heart. It is, however, the coloration that tells the story of the trinity. Heart of Jesus only comes in a trinity of colors: green, red, and white. The three colors represent the life of Jesus: green is the color of life, red is for the blood of Christ and white is the color of purity and surrender.

CALLICARPA AMERICANA

Also called: *Beautyberry or American Beautyberry*

The American Beautyberry is an eastern native shrub grown for its lavender or white berries that develop in the fall. Large clusters of attractive berries are born along the length of the Beautyberry stem. The American Beautyberry is a tough and durable woodland shrub that has been grown as an ornamental in eastern gardens for generations. The berries are edible in small quantities, and have been used externally as a mosquito repellant.

Native American folklore says that the Beautyberry was used as a medicinal herb, used to treat insect bites and skin ailments.

The foliage of the American Beautyberry is somewhat football shaped, matte green and heavily textured. The foliage is dense to the outside and sparser to the inside. Whether in the sun or in the shade, American Beautyberry will bring traditional ornamental value to the Southern garden.

CALYCANTHUS FLORIDUS

Also called: *Carolina Allspice, Sweet Shrub, or Bosom's Blossom*

Of all the common names for Calycanthus, Bosom's Blossom is the most interesting. An old wives tale from the Appalachian Mountains tells the tale of Bosom's Blossom. Women used to, in the days before regular bathing, put a Sweet Shrub blossom in their bosoms as a fragrance. These women hoped that the sweet scent would attract the attention of a young man who was suitable for marriage.

Carolina Allspice is native to the Southeastern United States. Native plant enthusiasts love this cold hardy shrub. A Calycanthus shrub can get over six feet tall and will sucker quite regularly, forming a colony. These colonies can be left to spread or dug up in clumps and easily transplanted. Sweet Shrub, as some gardeners call it, produces a sweet smelling burgundy colored flower in mid-spring through the summer. In autumn the large leaves of the Carolina Allspice turn bright yellow with a hint of gold.

Although Camellias are native to China and Southeast Asia, they are grown across the Southern United States for their ornamental value. This large evergreen shrub produces spectacular flowers in the winter months when few other things are blossoming. The award winning flowers range in color from pure white to deep red, with a couple of burgundy to lavender introductions. The flowers can be miniature in size or quite large.

Camellia shrubs are a Southern garden classic, having been featured in Southern gardens at least since 1802, where they are noted in historical records of Charleston, South Carolina.

Camellia interest waned after the Civil War, but took on new life after the turn-of-the-twentieth century. Camellia shows became popular in the 1930s and 40s and, in 1945, the American Camellia Society was formed. It has now grown to 4,000 members in forty-four states and twenty-two foreign countries with a permanent headquarters in Fort Valley, Georgia. A Quarterly Journal and a Camellia Yearbook are respected worldwide for their information on camellia culture, research, and new varieties.

Camellias were named in posthumous honor of George Joseph Kamel by Carolus Linnaeus, the Swedish botanist who developed the binomial system of nomenclature or the two name naming system of plants that is still in use today.

Also called: *Pepper*

The Pepper family is grown in the United States as a food crop, and to a lesser extent, an ornamental plant. Americans call the Capsicum by several names that include: Bell Pepper, Chili Pepper, Jalapeño, Habanero, and Banana. They are a popular vegetable garden plant, but peppers are actually a fruit. Pepper plants do have small but attractive flowers that develop into the fruit. There are several smaller varieties of Peppers that are grown strictly as ornamental plants, which can add color to the smaller garden.

The relatively mild Bell Peppers are the most popular by far and include yellow, red, and green varieties. They are used primarily for salads and crudités.

Jalapeños and Habaneros are "hotter" than Bell Peppers, and are used in sauces, stews, and chili. They are popular in Mexican and Cuban cooking.

Peppers are consumed both raw and cooked. They can be dried and used as a decoration in bunches. They can also be ground into a powder to make what is commonly referred to as "chili powder."

The heat of Peppers is a measurement of the amount of Capsaicin it contains. The heat is measured on the Scoville scale, using Scoville heat units (SHU). For example, a Bell Pepper rates at O SHU, whereas a Cayenne Pepper rates at 30,000 to 50,000 SHU and a law enforcement grade Pepper spray rates at 5,000,000 to 5,300,000 SHU.

*C*ARYA ILLINOINENSIS

Also called: *Pecan*

Most Americans know the Pecan as a culinary nut. Americans have enjoyed raw Pecans and many different kinds of Pecan desserts for generations. Pecans, like the fruit of all other members of the Hickory family, are not true nuts but a drupe. A drupe is a fruit with a fleshy outside shell and seed inside the shell. A Peach is another example of a drupe. The catkins or flowers emerge in the spring and are dangling tassel like structures. The bark develops deep fissures and rich texture with age, giving this tree a great deal of character.

Stories about the Pecan tree go back to the nation's earliest days. Thomas Jefferson planted trees he called "Illinois nut" in his orchard at Monticello. George Washington reported in his journal that Thomas Jefferson gave him "Illinois nuts," or Pecans, which Washington then planted at Mount Vernon, his Virginia home. Ever since the early colonial days of America, the Pecan has been a staple of our collective diets, providing early settlers with an important protein source. The colonists learned about the Pecan tree from the Native Americans who had harvested this nut for thousands of years.

The Pecan tree is a large, vase-shaped, deciduous shade tree that is native to the eastern half of the United States, growing from Texas to Pennsylvania and from Illinois to Florida. The modern landscaper knows that the Pecan tree is best reserved for large settings, such as parks or farms, to give it room to mature.

The state tree of Texas, the Pecan tree is slow-growing and can take up to twenty years to bear fruit. The leaves of the Pecan are compound and strongly falcate, a distinguishing identification feature.

CASSIA SENNA

Also called: *Cassia or Senna*

Cassia is a medium sized shrub that flowers profusely in the autumn. Its golden yellow flowers strongly resemble a Phalaenopsis Orchid. Sennas are also popular with gardeners for their unique ability to fold up their leaves at night, only to open again in the morning. They do best in full sun with regular water. Cassias will die back in the winter in Atlanta, but return each spring to look wonderful again.

Cassia is having a bit of a taxonomical identity crisis. Horticulturists are not sure whether to put them in the Genus Cassia or the Genus Senna, so both names are used. Cassias and Sennas are both Legumes, so either way it is in the Legume, or bean, family. Gardeners tend to accept either name as correct.

CENTRANTHUS RUBER

Also called: *Jupiter's Beard or Red Valerian*

This western perennial is a favorite among gardeners in Arizona, California, Nevada, and Utah. Jupiter's Beard is rare in North Georgia gardens, but it shouldn't be. The Centranthus boasts large rounded inflorescences of red flowers in mid spring and early summer at The State Botanical Gardens in Athens.

According to a Roman mythological legend, Jupiter was the supreme god and associated with love. Jupiter was also thought to have a full red beard, the color and symbol of love. The story of Jupiter's Beard says that wherever Jupiter laid his head for the night, a Jupiter's Beard flower would spring up and grow in that spot. The story reminds us to spread love wherever we go and if we do, love and justice will thrive.

Jupiter's Beard is a two-foot tall perennial and will self seed with little care. It can grow in the sun or shade, but it is not invasive. With minimal care Jupiter's Beard will provide the North Georgia gardener years of red flowers. Some gardeners know this garden plant by its other common name Red Valerian because it is in the Valerian family, but only distantly related to the medicinal herb Valerian.

$\mathcal{C}$HASMANTHIUM LATIFOLIUM

Also called: *Inland Sea Oats or Northern Sea Oats*

Northern Sea Oats are an upright clump forming native ornamental grass with somewhat bamboo-like foliage. Dangling seed heads hang in flat, long clusters from strongly arching stems. Flat green leaves turn copper in fall and the seed heads emerge green but turn purplish bronze in the late summer. Northern Sea Oats, in early winter, dry to a dull straw color. Clumping perennial grasses, like Northern Sea Oats, provide nesting sites and winter cover for quail and other small birds. The seeds also provide fall and winter food for a number of birds including Cardinals, Towhees, Sparrows and Finches as well as Squirrels and Chipmunks.

Northern Sea Oats have been known to hunters and country dwellers of the Eastern United States for generations, but only recently has it begun to be used in urban gardens. Many modern urban gardeners are looking for native ornamental grasses that are suitable for the smaller garden and the Northern Sea oat is perfect in those conditions. This grass tops out at about three feet high and two feet wide, but can be smaller. Unlike most native grasses, Inland Sea Oats are well suited for the shade, but can also be grown in full sun. It is not fussy about its conditions nor is it invasive. Inland Sea Oats provides nearly year-round interest, both to the gardener and to the wildlife. Cut Inland Sea Oats, a perennial, to the ground in mid-March to spur new spring growth. Despite the name "Oats," Inland Sea Oats are only distantly related to the cereal grain Oats (*Avena Sativa*).

CHIONANTHUS

Also called: *Granddad's Grey Beard or White Goddess Flower*

Chionanthus is ubiquitous in northern Europe and the British Isles where it has been held sacred by Pagans and Christians alike for centuries. The Chionanthus, with its loosely clustered pure white flowers was, for these religious traditions, a sure sign of summer's return.

Chionanthus led May Day celebrations as late as the 1920s along the Welsh border, being placed over doors of house and stable. A Chepstow resident told a local reporter in 1924: "My father used to do that, and also put some White Goddess flowers in each seed bed to make null and void the witches and the spells."

The link between Chionanthus and May Day was weakened by the calendar changes of 1752, after which Chionanthus was rarely in flower on May Day. But in Suffolk, anyone able to bring in a branch of white flowering Chionanthus on May Day morning won a bowl of cream for breakfast.

Chionanthus remains portentous: 'Harvest follows thirteen weeks after white flowers scents the air', is the Scottish farmers' belief. The well known 'Cast not a clout, till May be out', is often taken to refer to this late May flowering shrub, but probably actually refers to the sacred month of the White Goddess.

In the Christian tradition, the pure white flowers of the Chionanthus is seen as a symbol of purity and rejuvenation.

Most American gardeners are familiar with Chionanthus as Chionanthus Virginicus or Granddad's Grey Beard, although there are several varieties. Granddad's Grey Beard is an old-fashioned garden tree, planted long before the landscape industry. It is also a Southeastern native plant that attracts birds, squirrels and a host of other wildlife. Granddad's Grey Beard has bright clear yellow fall color.

CLERODENDRON

Also called: *Peanut Butter Plant*

The large leaves and close-knit flowers of the Clerodendron make it a must for an Atlanta area container garden with a tropical feel. The Clerodendron is a tropical flowering perennial that will need to be brought inside over winter in North Georgia.

In Macon and points south, it is a tender perennial that will, with mulch, return each year to grace the Southern garden with tropical charm.

The flowers are quite noticeable and greatly appreciated in the gardening world, but its leaves are what hold the secret. The back of the leaves, when lightly scratched, has the scent of peanut butter.

CLINOPODIUM GEORGIANUM

Also called: *Georgia Savory*

Georgia Savory is a relatively unknown plant to Georgia gardeners, but it shouldn't be. A small mostly evergreen shrub, Georgia Savory is round in form and somewhat stiff in texture. It vaguely resembles a Yaupon Holly in size and shape, but is more irregular in its branching. During the summer months into fall, it is covered in very small Mint family shaped flowers with colors ranging from white to light pink. Like all members of the Mint family, Georgia Savory has contrasting colored speckles on the inside of its flower petals. It is closely related to many widely used culinary herbs such as Basil, Mint, Rosemary, Sage, Marjoram, Oregano, Thyme, Lavender, and Perilla. In culinary terms, the word savory means not sweet, and such is the case with Georgia Savory.

For the North Georgia gardener, the Clinopodium will make a unique landscape plant or a fun addition to an existing full sun garden. Georgia Savory should be in every Georgia garden, if for no other reason than its name.

CONVALLARIA

Also called: Our Lady's Tears, Lily of the Valley, or May Flower

In Christian legend, the flower of the Convallaria is known as Our Lady's Tears, in reference to the tears that Mary shed at the crucifixion of her son Jesus. The legend says that Mary's tears turned into the Convallaria flower as they fell onto the blades of grass at the base of the cross.

According to a French mythological legend, there lived a holy man named St. Leonard, who lived in 559 C.E., in the Vienne Valley near Limoges. He renounced all worldly things and lived like a hermit in the depths of the woods. A dragon also lived there, and terrible battles took place between them. The dragon was driven further and further back into the woods toward the edge of the forest, until finally it disappeared altogether, leaving St. Leonard the conqueror. The places of their battles are marked by beds of Convallaria that sprang up wherever the ground was sprinkled with the blood of St. Leonard.

In the Language of flowers, the Lily of the Valley signifies sweetness and the renewal of happiness. Because of its association with purity and love, Lily of the Valley became the national flower of Finland in 1967.

Despite its mythical powers, all parts of the Convallaria plant are considered poisonous.

COREOPSIS

Also called: *Tickseed*

What started out as a wildflower has now become one of the most beloved garden perennials in America. The Coreopsis is a yellow spring to summer flower in the Aster family.

According to a South American flower legend, the Coreopsis was one of the flowers of the sun gods. Ancient peoples of Brazil believed that the Coreopsis, growing wild in their fields, were the commands of the gods. They believed that to cut down a Coreopsis was to disobey the wishes of the gods.

One legend tells of Tick, a young Brazilian man who thought that the Coreopsis was the most beautiful flower he had ever seen. He cut it down to make a flower arrangement to take to the young woman he was courting. He told her that while the flower was indeed beautiful, her radiance outshined the bright gold flower. She was horrified that Tick had disobeyed the commandment of the sun gods to leave the Coreopsis in the fields. She became frightened and angry at Tick, fearing the wrath of the gods. This is why today we have the saying "Ticked off!" to express anger.

Also called: *Dogwood*

An old Christian legend has it that, in the time of Jesus, the Dogwood was the size of the Oak trees and other kings of the forest. Because of its massive, strong, and straight trunk, it was selected as the timber for the cross to be used to crucify Jesus. The Dogwood tree was sad at being used for such a purpose, and asked Jesus for forgiveness. The crucified Jesus, in his gentle pity for the sorrow of the Dogwood, said to it, "Because of your sorrow and understanding for my suffering, never again will the Dogwood tree grow large and strong enough to be used as a cross." Henceforth it was slender, bent, and small. The legend explains why its blossoms are in the form of a cross — two long and two short petals of pure white. At the outer edge of each petal there are nail prints stained with red to represent Christ's blood, and in the center of the flower there is a crown of gold.

The Dogwoods pictured here can be seen in all their seasonal glory. The large white blossoms come out in the spring signaling the arrival of warmer weather, while the gentle burgundy red fall color and bright berries signal cooler days. The Dogwood is a great tree for the North Georgia gardener with its traditional look, manageable size and exceptional seasonal attributes.

*C*UPRESSUS ARIZONICA

Also called: *Arizona Cypress*

A magnificent conifer, the Arizona Cypress is the only conifer that is native to the Southwestern United States. Its overall form is upright with a strong central trunk. It is slender and conical in shape, but will become rounder with age. The leaves of the Arizona Cypress are evergreen, scale like, resembling a bullwhip handle. The leaves can be resinous. They are gray green to silvery blue and are often quite glaucous.

The Arizona Cypress flower is monoecious, meaning male and female flowers on the same plant. The male flowers are small, pale yellow green at the ends of the branch tips, while female flowers are near the branch tips. The flowers are typically too small for the naked eye to see, but can be photographed with the right equipment.

Like all conifers, the Arizona Cypress produces a cone or fruit. It is dry, round and woody. They are one inch in diameter, with six or seven pointed scales. The cone matures in two years and may stay attached for several years.

The bark of the Arizona Cypress is considered to be very attractive. It shreds and peels in long strips to reveal gray and reddish brown sections. As the tree ages, the bark may develop a fine, shallow furrowed pattern or reveal patchy characteristics. Despite the Arizona Cypress being a desert tree, it does well in North Georgia.

In Native American culture, the Arizona Cypress was considered sacred. One legend says that if the spirit bird returned to the Cypress tree, then there was water in the area and that hunting would be abundant that year. If the tree had no birds, then the cones of the Cypress would fall like rain, and the cones were to be that year's harvest.

Other Native American legends tell of how the Arizona Cypress was used to build ladders and tools. It is said in legend that a ceremonial game was played using the ball like cones.

CYCLAMEN

Also called: *Cyclamen or Sowbread*

Pliny the Elder, an ancient Roman naturalist and writer, recommended Cyclamen for every household. "Where it grows no noxious spells can have effect," he wrote. The Cyclamen's ear-like shape made it a natural choice for charlatans to use in treating aural complaints. Cyclamen was the choice plant for drinkers across Europe, because, it was said, even a little added to wine increased intoxication.

It played its part in love stories of old, but a pregnant woman who stepped on it might suffer a miscarriage if she did not quickly replant it and have its flowers for a garland around her neck when she gave birth.

In Southern Spain, pigs have been known to like it, giving it an alternative name of "Sowbread" in that country.

Despite these rather quirky stories, Cyclamens make great houseplants year round or annuals outside in the Atlanta border. They require similar growing conditions as Orchids, with a small commitment of time returning rewards of fascinating foliage and bright petal colors all season. Cyclamens are the perfect companion plant for Ferns and Cast Iron Plants, as they all require shade and moisture.

DAHLIA

Dahlia is a popular garden flower, grown for its bright colors and full blossoms. Dahlias are native to Central America, and are the national flower of Mexico. Botanists have formally recognized them since the early seventeenth century.

Dahlias can be annuals or perennials depending on growing conditions. They prefer full sun and somewhat dry soil. Most varieties of Dahlias need to be dug up in the late fall and over-wintered, although some will survive in the ground. Dahlia flowers are insect pollinated.

Dahlias are a flower show favorite, and many competitions are conducted across the country each year. At these flower shows, many new cultivars that were produced the previous year are introduced, judged and made available to the public. Dahlias are one of the most photographed flowers seen in the garden today.

DAUCUS CAROTA

Also called: *Queen Anne's Lace*

The flat round flower cluster of Queen Anne's Lace can be seen floating above lacy leaves in gardens and across fields all over North Georgia. While most people think of Queen Anne's Lace as a weed, it has a centuries' old tradition of being used as a cut flower in arrangements. Queen Anne's Lace has also been historically used as a wedding flower, its white color symbolizing purity.

Daucus Carota is related to the carrot and, when pulled up, has a strong scent of a carrot. Although a relative of the carrot, the long pale white root is not generally eaten.

DECUMARIA BARBARA

Also called: *Woodvamp*

Woodvamp is a shade loving evergreen vine in the Hydrangea family, and is noted among native plant enthusiasts as one of only a few Southeastern United States native vines. It does need a wall, trellis or other support to grow on and is generally considered well behaved in the garden.

A small white flower appears in the spring, but the Woodvamp flower is not long lasting and most gardeners grow it for its glossy deep green foliage.

DELPHINIUM

Also called: *Larkspur*

An elegant flowering annual in the summer color border, Delphiniums are one of the gardener's few choices for blue blossoms. Waves of dark green, fully serrated foliage are accented with huge spikes of tall, usually blue purple flowers in mid-summer. Because of their height and dramatic appearance, Delphiniums are almost always planted in groups at the back of the border. Most varieties available to the North Georgia gardener are annuals. Perennial varieties of Delphiniums are available online through seed sources. The botanical name Delphinium comes from the Greek word for Dolphin, referring, most likely, to the petal and sepal configuration. The common name Larkspur comes from the flower arrangement. Larkspur flowers are pollinated by both butterflies and bees. They are a standard in English cottage style gardens.

Delphiniums thrive in areas with relatively warm summers with plenty of rain. They struggle in dry summer conditions. Delphiniums are available in a wide range of sizes, from less than two feet tall to over six feet. Flower colors include blue, purple, red, white, and yellow. The rich, bright blues are considered especially desirable by most gardeners. The Delphinium begin flowering in late spring or early summer and continue well into the fall. The flowers are often used in dried flower arrangements or for arts and craft projects. In the western United States, the Larkspur is known as a self-seeding meadow wildflower.

In France, scholars who were taxing their eyes over volumes of text were advised to keep the Larkspur flower on their desks and to glance at it often. To look at the mid-summer fires through bunches of Larkspur meant trouble free vision for the year to come.

DICENTRA

Also called: *Bleeding Heart*

A shade loving plant, Bleeding Heart is an old fashioned favorite among gardeners in both Europe and America. While its leaves resemble those of the Peony, Bleeding heart is grown for its heart shaped flowers that dangle in neat rows below their stem.

Bleeding Heart flowers come in white, pink, or red and look very delicate. The Bleeding Heart is not, however, delicate. It is quite a robust perennial in the Atlanta area garden. Even with the coldest winters and the hottest summers, Dicentra looks great year after year with very little fuss.

Many gardeners like to divide their perennials every few years, to either clean out a flowerbed or to give away to friends at plant swaps. Dicentra, with its natural ability to fill in an area, makes a perfect plant to occasionally divide and give away. The best time to divide a Dicentra is in the spring after new growth begins or late in the fall as the foliage is dying down. Be sure to water well upon transplanting, followed by fish emulsion a few weeks later.

DIGITALIS

Also called: *Foxglove*

A summer blossoming perennial, Foxglove prefers a shady spot in the Garden. A tall flower spike develops from a rather nondescript rosette of wrinkled matte green leaves as the weather gets hotter. This flower spike bares a cascading whirl of tubular shaped flowers that always have speckles of an opposing color on the inside.

In Symbology, Foxglove flowers have both positive and negative meanings. They are said to sometimes harm and sometimes heal. In the language of flowers, Foxglove is associated with insincerity. The common name is said to come from the earlier name Fox's Glove, meaning the sly hand of the fox.

In other accounts, a more positive aspect of Foxglove is recorded. In European medieval gardens that were dedicated to Mother Mary, Foxglove was called Our Lady's Gloves or Gloves of the Virgin. This is said to mean the hand of the Mother Mary is the hand of comfort and healing.

$\mathcal{E}$ CHEVERIA

Also called: *Hens & Chicks*

Echeveria is a flowering succulent native to Mexico. Most gardeners know it as Hens & Chicks, referring to its habit of producing offsets (or Chicks) around the base of the mother plant. After the mother plant flowers, it dies and one of the offsets takes over and starts the cycle again. The offsets are easily removed manually and used to start new plants. Hens & Chicks is identifiable by its tightly configured rosette of thick fleshy leaves that come in a wide range of colors and patterns.

Echeveria can withstand full sun and temperature extremes, but does poorly in soil that is too moist. It is most often seen growing in pots and container gardening. Hens & Chicks is in the Crassulaceae family and is a close relative of the Jade plant.

ECHINACEA

Also called: *Coneflower*

Echinacea is a classic garden perennial. Although this North American native wildflower has been grown domestically for generations, it can still be seen growing wild across America. All Coneflowers are in the Aster family, as are the Sunflowers.

Because it is an American flower, it could not have been the flower of which the poet Ovid tells. When in Ovid's epic poem Metamorphoses, Clytie, dying of grief at her desertion by the Sun god Helios, was turned into a flower, the blossom was probably a more modest one.

One tale from the Pagan tradition tells of Ecken, who, every spring, invoked the Coneflower. He tried to entice it to bring the warmth of summer back to the frozen land. Each year, slowly, the warmth of the summer grew along with the Coneflower. But the gods of winter, favoring the Holly, eventually overthrew the Coneflower, and the Coneflower went down while the Holly had its months. The Coneflower so loved Ecken for his efforts to save its life that the Coneflower named itself Echinacea in honor of Ecken. Some say the battle between Ecken and the gods of winter continues to this day.

ℰLAEAGNUS

Also called: *Ugly Agnes or Silverberry*

Silverberry is a large arching to almost weeping evergreen shrub. It flowers in the fall and early winter, but the flowers are small and most gardeners favor the sweet fragrance. Some varieties produce a small reddish fruit that dangles down from the long arching branches. The fruit is edible, but considered bland by most standards.

Despite the low-key flowers and fruit, the Elaeagnus has many fine qualities. The leaves, flowers and fruit are covered with silver to honey colored speckles. It quickly makes a large, thick and beautiful barrier type hedgerow. Although it takes

pruning well, the Silverberry shows best when given room to spread. Gardeners who let it grow naturally will be rewarded with an outstanding shrub in a few short years. The overall shape and texture, with age, are regular and uniform, yet flowing and natural. Silverberry is a tough shrub, withstanding heat, cold and neglect.

The Silverberry shrub attracts a variety of birds and other wildlife. Birds eat the berries and build nests in its branches, while the flowers attract bees and butterflies. Squirrels nest under its canopy for shelter in winter.

$\mathcal{E}$QUISETUM HYEMALE

Also called: *Horsetail Rush*

Horsetail Rush is not a true Rush, but more closely related to ferns. Equisetum Hyemale is the last remaining species in the genus, and is a plant that dates back thousands of years.

Horsetail Rush is a reed like perennial in the bog or water garden. The evergreen stems are cylindrical, hollow, usually unbranched, and have rough longitudinal ridges. Its shape can be compared to that of a straw. The tiny leaves are joined together around the one-third inch diameter stem, forming a narrow dark band or sheath around each joint. It does not flower, but rather produces spores with which to reproduce. Horsetail Rush spreads and forms colonies by shallow rhizomes, or underground stems, and is easily propagated by dividing the clumps and replanting immediately.

A Roman military story from the last century B.C.E. tells us of how the soldiers used the Horsetail Rush to surprise their enemy. Soldiers would use a piece of Horsetail Rush like a snorkeling device, enabling them to breathe and move around under water undetected. The piece of Horsetail Rush simply blended in with all the other Reeds and Rushes along the water's edge. This allowed the soldiers to infiltrate areas where they would not normally be able to gain access.

$\mathcal{E}$UCALYPTUS

Also called: *Gum Tree*

Eucalyptus is an enormous genus of plants in the Myrtle family. They range from small shrubs to massive trees. Most members of the Eucalyptus genus are native to Australia, but are now grown all over the world. In many parts of the world, the Eucalyptus is known as the Gum Tree.

Although Eucalyptus plants are used for timber and for their oils in Australia and across the Mediterranean region, most Americans grow Eucalyptus shrubs and trees for their ornamental value. Some varieties of Eucalyptus are planted for their flowers, but most often their leaves, bark and overall structure are the desirable features. Eucalyptus trees provide the landscape a unique leaf and bark texture. Like the unrelated Crape Myrtle, most types of Eucalyptus have a smooth peeling bark that is a muted grey, highlighted with brown, pink, green or cream coloration. The bark of most species becomes more furrowed and rougher in texture with age. The dangling evergreen leaves are usually lanceolate, that is, long and slender with a sharply pointed apex.

Koalas, a marsupial native to Australia, live in and feed almost exclusively on the leaves of the Eucalyptus.

EUONYMUS ALATUS

Also called: *Burning Bush, Winged Spindle, or Spindle*

Burning Bush is a strongly upright multi branched shrub. The most unique feature of the Burning Bush is its four raised corky ridges or "wings" that extend along the length of the stems. These corky ridges are not bark in the true sense of the word, but do offer the plant some protection. The botanical name Alata or Alatus, in the plural, is the Latin word for wing. The botanical name Euonymus is Greek in origin, although the Euonymus is native to China.

Euonymus Alatus is named Burning Bush because of its fall color. Burning Bush is a great fall color addition to any sunny spot, lighting up the bed or hedgerow with light salmon to deep red color from early October through Thanksgiving. Burning Bush will lose its leaves by early December.

Euonymus wood was traditionally used in England and the Netherlands for making spindles for spinning wheels. This is the origin of the common English name for the shrub. In Europe, Euonymus is known as Spindle.

$\mathscr{E}$UPHORBIA MILII

Also called: *Crown of Thorns*

Crown of Thorns is a thorny, rigid succulent with deep salmon to red flowers. Many Americans know Crown of Thorns as a houseplant, but Southern gardeners can grow it outside with some winter protection.

Although native to Madagascar, the Crown of Thorns was thought to have been brought to the Middle East before the time of Christ.

According to a legend from the Christian tradition, Euphorbia Milii was the plant that the Romans used to make the crown that was put on Jesus' head during the crucifixion. The legend also says that the blood of Christ ran onto the once pure white flowers and forever stained them red. This legend is where we get the plant's common name Crown of Thorns. There are several other plants in folklore that also claim this name for the same reason. The truth is lost to history.

$\mathcal{E}$UTROCHIUM

Also called: *Joe Pye Weed*

Ubiquitous along the country roads and abandoned fields of North Georgia, Joe Pye Weed is as old fashioned and all-American as garden plants can be. For as long as America has been America, Joe Pye Weed has been gracing dinner tables and driving butterflies crazy.

While some gardeners' think of Joe Pye Weed as weedy, with easy care requirements and the most distinct pale purple flowers, most gardeners think of Joe Pye Weed as a future gift to a fellow gardener.

There are several varieties of Joe Pye Weed, ranging from dwarf selections to ones over five feet tall. All varieties have a large flat flower head that is a muted, almost pale, purple. Joe Pye Weed is a reliable perennial and a must for any native or butterfly gardener.

ℱARFUGIUM JAPONICA (FORMERLY LIGULARIA)

Also called: *Leopard Plant or Yellowdots*

The shade garden can hold many secrets and surprises for the plant enthusiast. Hidden away under the shadows of grand trees lies a world of plants that cannot bare the light of day. Such residents of this shady place are Hostas, Ferns, and Farfugium. Though no one can explain exactly where the common name Leopard Plant comes from, it most likely has to do with the yellow spots that grace the surface of this large leaved perennial.

While most gardeners grow Leopard Plant for its foliage, it does occasionally produce a flower inflorescence, an upright raceme of golden yellow. It may be grown as a single specimen, in arrangements or as a low growing groundcover. Like many shade plants, it displays well in mass plantings. Yellowdots needs a fair amount of water, but be sure to water it from the ground, as water sitting on the foliage can cause unwanted rot.

Farfugium is a large family, with many varieties. They are all native to Japan.

$\mathcal{F}$OENICULUM VULGARE

Also called: *Fennel*

Fennel is an herb garden standard around the world. It is grown for its feathery foliage and culinary uses. Fennel can be grown for its bright yellow flowers, but this is rare. Fennel is a biennial and will flower only in its second year.

Cooks have made good use of Fennel over the centuries for its sweet licorice flavor that can be used as a fresh garnish or as an ingredient to add freshness to many dishes.

Black Swallowtail butterfly larvae feed on this herb in the summer months, and many gardeners grow it simply to attract butterflies.

FOTHERGILLA

Also called: *Witch Wand*

Fothergilla is a spring flowering shrub that is native to the Southeastern United States. Its puffy, brushy and rounded white flowers emerge in April or May and persist through the summer. Fothergilla can grow to a height of seven feet, but is usually smaller. The Fothergilla has a stout, upright, heavily branched structure and should never need pruning.

Fothergilla is also grown for its outstanding fall color. A medium green over the summer, the heavily textured leaves turn many shades of red and salmon in early October. In some species, hues of yellow and gold compliment the reds.

Fothergilla gets its other common name, Witch Wand, from an old farmer's tale that says it was once used by witches of the fields to make their wands. Being in the Hamamelis family, Witch Wand is a close relative of Witch Hazel and many stories surrounding them have been used interchangeably. There is also mention of forest elves using the Witch Wand as a rod or staff to drive out unwanted spirits from the trees.

${\mathcal{F}}$UCHSIA

The Fuchsia is one of the most outstanding hanging basket flowers in the Atlanta area. The Fuchsias rich red, pink and fuchsia colors brighten any porch or deck throughout the summer months. The blossoms cascade down the sides of the baskets, reaching down two feet or more.

While most hanging basket flowers are annuals that die in the winter, Fuchsias can be brought inside during cold weather. They need only to be cut back and watered sparingly to make it through the winter indoors. In the spring, after frost has passed, they may be put back outside, fertilized and enjoyed again for another season.

All Fuchsias are native to tropical Southeastern Asia. In its native area Fuchsia is thought to represent the lovers' heart, and is given as a romance flower.

GAURA

Also called: *Gauri or Whirling Butterflies*

Whirling butterflies are a beautiful, tough and long lasting flower in the sunny border. Many small butterfly-like flowers sway in the wind, floating on what seems like air above a swirling rosette of mounded luscious green to burgundy leaves. Gaura flowers come in white and several shades of pink.

While they seem like they are floating, the Whirling Butterfly flowers are actually suspended on slim arching and leafless stems about two to six feet long. Whirling Butterfly is a spring blossoming flower, emerging in late April and lasting until the first hard frost. They are a reliable perennial in the Southern garden.

Gaura has been grown in India for centuries, and is an integral part of a Hindu marriage festival known as The Gauri Festival.

During the first year after her marriage, every new bride in India celebrates continuing festivals with great enthusiasm. Almost every festival sees the bride back with her parents to relive the joys of her childhood with her friends. Festive days are her chance to entertain her friends, get to know her new relatives and to bring her own and her new husband's families together with a sense of joy and celebration. During the festivals, both of her families pamper her with gifts of clothing and jewelry.

One celebration that is specifically for her is the worship of the goddess Gauri, performed once a week in the month of Shravan. Gauri is a festive manifestation of the goddess Parvati. The idol of the goddess Gauri is displayed with ceremony and ritual, and is offered jewelry, fruits, and flowers. The symbol of Gauri, the Gaura flower, is presented to the goddess.

Its butterfly form represents the new bride coming out from childhood into her adult beauty and new life as a married woman.

Gaura flowers are also placed at the entrance of the home for visitors, for they too are going through the transformation of their friend from child to adult. All this creates an atmosphere of serenity in the home. Women from the family get together with friends of all ages and spend the night playing games, dancing, singing, and eating the feast made for the occasion. Bangles, Gaura flowers, and other adornments are given to all of the women present. The celebrations are a time of fun for every young girl. In Indian culture women are expected to be a combination of both strength and beauty, as symbolized by the Gaura flower.

The goddess Gauri, after staying for a month at the parental home, is supposed to depart. The departing is naturally with a heavy heart and leaving the others, too, in a similar mood. All that is to remain of the festival is the sweet memories and the hope for a new life as a married woman.

$\mathcal{G}$ELSEMIUM SEMPERVIRENS

Also called: *Carolina Jasmine or Yellow Jessamine*

Carolina Jasmine is an evergreen vine with bright yellow trumpet shaped flowers. The flowers blossom in abundance twice a year, in the spring and in the fall. In a sheltered location it can flower from spring until the first frost. The Carolina Jasmine has long, thin-arching stems that need support. This flowering vine, with its tangling compact habit has become a favorite on fences and mailboxes.

Carolina Jasmine is the state flower of South Carolina, and is a Southeastern native. Gelsemium Sempervirens is a tough and durable plant that needs little attention once it is established. It can easily survive frost and frequent light freezes, but may die under prolonged exposure to freezing conditions. Beware: all parts of this plant are poisonous.

Also called: *Silverbell or Snowdrop Tree*

Silverbell is a large shrub or small tree that flowers white in late spring. The flowers of the Silverbell dangle beneath the branches in small loose clusters of three or four flowers. When the Halesia is in full flower, it appears to be covered in snow, hence the common name Snowdrop Tree.

The bright green leaves are also in clusters along the length of the branches, similar to the Crabapple tree. The Silverbell's leaves last late into the season, but it is a deciduous shrub. The branch structure is loose and open, meandering freely up to the sun. The Silverbell is an old fashioned favorite, having been available long before the modern garden center. For the organic native gardener, the Silverbell is a nearly perfect plant. It is native to the eastern United States and it is completely disease-resistant and pest free, never needing to be sprayed or treated with chemicals.

HEDERA CANARIENSIS

Also called: *Algerian Ivy or Canary Island Ivy*

Algerian Ivy is a large leafed relative of the common English Ivy. Hedera Canariensis is native to the Canary Islands, off the coast of northwest Africa. The botanical name Hedera comes from the Greek word Helix, meaning twist or curve. It refers to the twisting nature of the stems.

The Canary Island Ivy is used by most gardeners as a ground cover in a shady to part sunny location. Like the common English Ivy, it can be slow to get started, but will show visible growth in a few years. Remember the old garden saying about the Ivies: First year it sleeps, second year it creeps and third year it leaps!

Canary Island Ivy has large showy evergreen leaves that come in both green and variegated varieties. It does not flower reliably, and is grown for its foliage. This vine can be invasive, but is generally not thought to be a nuisance.

HELENIUM

An old garden notion says that sneezeweed's bright yellow and gold flowers were once gathered in late fall and hung to dry. The dried petals were then ground into a powder that was to be snorted, therefore making the person sneeze profusely. It was thought that the powder had magical powers that would make one sneeze out the evil winter spirits. Once the spirits were gone, a healthy and warm winter was to prevail.

Another tale about Helenium tells the story of Helen's Flower. There was a girl in the 1920s who loved to tend her garden. Helen would get up every morning and weed and water the flowerbeds before school. When summer came and school ended, Helen was happy, because this meant she could have all day to tend her garden. She worked hard and was proud of the beautiful flowers and shrubs that her garden produced, but she became lonely for friends to play with. She spent so much time in the garden she had forgotten how to have fun with the other children. It was late in the summer when Helen began to cry about the friendships she had missed out on. Her tears fell on the garden soil and the Helenium began to grow.

It wasn't long before another little girl came walking down the sidewalk and stopped to see what Helen was crying about. Helen told the other little girl, named Kate, that she had wasted her summer in the garden and lost out on friendship, and that all she had to show for her labor was this one bunch bright yellow flowers.

The other little girl looked at the flowers and said that they were beautiful and that they would look perfect in the dollhouse that she had spent the summer building. The two girls took the flowers to Kate's room and arranged them in the dollhouse. Helen's flowers added a bright and cheerful glow to the miniature house. Both girls were happy to have someone to share their hobbies with, and the two girls went on to be lifelong friends.

HEUCHERA

Also called: *Coral Bells*

Most Coral Bell plants are grown for their rounded foliage, but they do flower nicely in the early summer. The small single white flower inflorescence sits up high above the deep burgundy or lime green foliage.

Coral Bells are shade or semi shade perennials from Macon northward over all of North Georgia. All Heucheras, regardless of type, are grown as short mounds of rosette-patterned foliage that come in a wide variety of colors, ranging from deep purple to bright lime. The mid range for coloring is a rich burgundy.

According to tradition, Coral Bells represent patience and a delicate nature. They are listed in the language of flowers as purity and reason. Coral Bells are also a popular wedding flower for table arrangements, noted for their long lasting beauty.

Heucheras are an easy care plant, needing only occasional watering and fish emulsion in the spring to give the gardener years of enjoyment.

HIBISCUS

Also called: *Rose of Sharon*

Hibiscus is a large plant family. Most members of the Hibiscus Family are tropical, but several varieties do well in the Atlanta area. They are mostly deciduous shrubs that bare large flowers in the summer months. The flowers of the Hibiscus come in a wide range of colors.

In folklore, the Hibiscus is associated with the Feminine side of personality. It is also the flower of Venus. According to the calendar of flowers the Hibiscus represents dreams and levitation.

HYDRANGEA QUERCIFOLIA

Also called: *Oakleaf Hydrangea*

The Oakleaf Hydrangea is truly North America's Hydrangea. It is native to the eastern United States and grows abundantly from Ontario to central Florida. Its rugged durability has long made it a favorite among native plant enthusiasts.

The flower of the Oakleaf Hydrangea is a large upright panicle with many individual robust pure white flowers. As the weather cools, the flowers die down but stay on the panicle and resemble a dried flower arrangement. Under good conditions these dried arrangements can stay on the Oakleaf until spring.

The Oakleaf Hydrangea's fall color is considered by many gardeners to be its best attribute. The large abundant Oak tree like leaves turn many shades of red to burgundy starting in mid October.

The Oakleaf Hydrangea is a semi-evergreen, meaning it loses most of its leaves in winter, but retains some of them. During the winter months the Oakleaf features a beautiful and outstanding branch structure and exfoliating bark pattern, especially as it ages.

Oak tree nymphs are said to inhabit this large shrub, even though it is not a true Oak tree.

$\mathcal{I}$LEX SSP.

Also called: *Holly*

The Holly is the classic old-fashioned landscape shrub. It's tough evergreen leaves and bright red berries have graced European and American gardens for centuries. There are many types of Hollies to choose from, everything from tall trees to small shrubs.

There are two main varieties of Hollies: the Cornuta, or large leafed Holly, which are native to China, and the Crenata, or small leafed Holly, which is native to Japan. Although native to China and Japan, Hollies have been grown all over the world for centuries.

In the pagan tradition, the Holly is a representation of the gods of winter. Because the Holly is an evergreen, it is thought to be alive and influential even in the dead of winter when most other gods are asleep in the underworld.

In the northern Celtic Pagan tradition, there is the story of The Celtic Holly King. The Holly, associated with the spirit of flora and the waning forces of nature, is personified as the mythological Holly King. He's usually portrayed as an old man adorned in winter clothing, wearing a Holly wreath on his head and holding a Holly branch stave. The Holly King rules nature during its waning time from Litha, the summer solstice, to Yule. During each solstice, he and his brother The Oak King engage in a contest for the goddess' attentions. The one who is victorious presides over the forest through the next half of the year.

KALMIA LATIFOLIA

Also called: *Mountain Laurel or Spoonwood*

An old fashioned flowering garden shrub, Mountain Laurel has been grown for its abundance of distinctive cup shaped flowers for generations. Mountain Laurel is an eastern United States native, ranging from New England to Southern Georgia west to Missouri. While the name Mountain Laurel implies that it is strictly a mountain shrub, it grows just as well in wide-open areas and across the Midwest. The entire shrub is poisonous to both farm animals and humans. It has been known to kill sheep that graze on it, leading to the names Calf-kill and Sheep-Kill.

In Native American folklore it is called Spoonwood because Native Tribes were said to have made spoons out of the wood. Given that Spoonwood is toxic, this is likely just lore rather than fact.

Carolus Linnaeus, the creator of the binomial system of nomenclature, named the genus Kalmia for the Finnish botanist Pehr Kalm. Mountain Laurel is in the plant family Ericaceae, making it a close relative of Rhododendrons, Azaleas, and Heaths.

Mountain Laurel is the state flower of both Connecticut and Pennsylvania.

KERRIA JAPONICA

Also called: *Japanese Yellow Rose or Yamabuki*

In the United States, Kerria is the most commonly used name for this small Japanese shrub, but some gardeners call it Japanese Yellow Rose. So named because this Rose family member is native to Japan.

Kerria is a short, open shrub that flowers on the ends of sprawling, loosely arching stems. Southern gardeners will note the similarity of the flower to Lady Banks Rose, although they blossom at different times. Kerria is an old fashioned garden plant that needs only full to part sun and average rainfall to look its best. The flowers come in single, double and full petal arrangement.

Yamabuki, as it is called in Japan, has a long tradition in the mountain culture. It is there that it is associated with Buddhist monks and the serenity of mountainous seclusion. The Yamabuki is also well represented in Japanese watercolor paintings and in Japanese poetry.

LILIUM

Also called: *Lily or Easter Lily*

According to an ancient Semitic legend, the Lily sprang from the tears of Eve when she was expelled from the Garden of Eden, having just found she was approaching motherhood. In later Christian folklore it was said that the Lily had been yellow until the day the Virgin Mary stooped to pick it up. In Christian symbolism the Lily represented purity, chastity and innocence, and is a symbol of resurrection and Easter. The white Madonna Lily was, in

antiquity, considered the special flower of the Holy Virgin, and during the Middle Ages it was almost invariably pictured in the subject of the annunciation placed in a vase standing by the queen of heaven. Easter Lily, to this day, holds a nearly sacred place in the Catholic tradition.

In modern times gardeners refer to this Lily as Easter Lily or Mother's Day Lily, and it is given at Easter and again at Mother's Day. The Lily can be grown in the garden as a resurrecting perennial, to be enjoyed year after year. Although white is the most popular color, it comes in several colors and patterns.

LIRIODENDRON TULIPIFERA

Also called: *Tulip Poplar or Tulip Tree*

When Europeans first settled North America, they found most types of transportation, such as horses, oxen, and wagons, to be useless. Forests covered the land from the Atlantic Ocean to the Mississippi River. The only truly accessible routes inland were the rivers and streams. Most waterways were difficult to explore by boat and explorers soon adopted the dugout canoe, a Native American form of transportation. Many of the early dugouts were made from the trunks of the Liriodendron Tulipifera.

Carolus Linnaeus, a Swiss botanist, named this large native tree the Liriodendron Tulipifera, or as he described it, "The Lily Tree that produces Tulips." The Lenni Lenape, a Native American tribe from Delaware, called it muxulhemenshi or the "tree from which canoes are made." Dugouts were made from a number of trees, but the Tulip Tree was one of the quickest from which to build a watercraft.

Tulip tree wood rotted rather quickly in water, therefore these dugouts typically lasted only one or two seasons. The massive size of the Tulip Trees provided natives, then explorers and later settlers with large canoes that could haul loads and maintain buoyancy in a shallow creek. The wood was workable with only fire and hatchets.

After losing a land grant in 1799, a Kentucky settlement felled a tulip tree and fashioned a sixty-foot dugout. Led by Daniel Boone, thirty-five people left Boonesborough, Kentucky, with their families and household goods. The women and children traveled in the hollowed-out tree while the men drove the livestock overland. Once they were in St. Louis, the Spanish welcomed Daniel Boone's group to the Western Territory. Boone's group was granted land on the banks of the Missouri River and the outcasts founded the first major American settlement in the West, with the Tulip Tree continuing to be a source of lumber for the fledgling colony.

The Tulip part of the Liriodendron Tulipifera's name comes from the Tulip like flower that it produces mid-spring. Tulip trees are deciduous, that is they lose their leaves in the winter. The Tulip Poplar is the state tree of both Kentucky and Tennessee.

LYCHNIS CHALCEDONICA

Also called: *Maltese Cross*

The Maltese Cross is the symbol of an order of Christian warriors known as the Knights of Malta. Through the Knights, the Maltese Cross came to be identified with the Mediterranean island of Malta and is now one of its national symbols. The Maltese Cross is displayed on the back of two new Euro coins from Malta.

The Maltese Cross is an eight-pointed cross and has the form of four V shaped arms joined together at their tips. In this configuration, each arm has two points. Its design is based on crosses used since the first crusades through the Mediterranean region.

The Maltese Cross flower gets its common name due to its strong resemblance to the Maltese Cross. The Maltese Cross is a deep red perennial flower in the summer garden. It is an herbaceous plant growing to three feet tall with unbranched stems. The leaves are produced in opposite pairs that are simple, broad, and lanceolate, one to four inches long. The one-inch wide flowers are produced on an upright inflorescence. The Maltese Cross flower has a five lobed corolla, with each lobe further split into two smaller lobes. The fruit is a capsule containing many seeds.

Just as other summer blossoming perennials are looking tired and stressed in the late summer border, the Lycoris Radiata appears showing bright red flowers on a leafless stalk. The ability of this old fashioned favorite to grow seemingly without leaves is where it gets the common name Naked Lady.

The unique flowers of the Red Spider Lily resemble the lily in many ways, but it is actually a member of the Amaryllis family. The bright red flowers are borne in loose radial clusters at the top of the stalk. The individual flowers are small, with the cluster being about six to nine inches across. Each flower produces six or seven stamens that lurch out about five inches from the flower center, leading to the name Red Spider Lily.

The Red Spider Lily is a bulb perennial that goes dormant in the heat of the summer months, flowers in the autumn, and then produces strap-like leaves after the flowers fade in the early winter. The leaves will need to be cut back in the late spring. The Red Spider Lily is very drought tolerant, needing only rainwater once established. The Red Spider Lily is native to Japan and China, although it has naturalized throughout the Southeastern United States.

In Japanese mythology the Lycoris is associated with autumn and death; in much the same way as the autumn season often signals the coming of death in English metaphorical vernacular. A Japanese legend says that one should never wish death upon another, for the holder of such anger will have Red Spider Lily flowers blossoming along behind them for as long as they hold that resentment.

In the Buddhist tradition, the Lycoris is used to celebrate autumn, and is often planted at the graves of ancestors to show respect.

 YSIMACHIA

Also called: *White Gooseneck Loosestrife or Creeping Jenny*

White Gooseneck Loosestrife is named after King Lysimachus of Italy. King Lysimachus discovered that Loosestrife, when tied to yokes of unruly oxen and horses, made them biddable and submissive. It deters flies and gnats, the reason for its success with animals. White Gooseneck Loosestrife is an old fashioned garden perennial that requires regular watering, hence its association with gnats. While it does drive away flies and gnats, it also spreads aggressively in a semi shade location. The name White Gooseneck Loosestrife is obvious from the shape and color of the flower.

Several names identify the light lime green leaves of Lysimachia. It is known as Creeping Jenny in America and Creeping Charlie in England. It also has the names Moneywort and Meadow Runner. Atlanta area gardeners know Creeping Jenny as a reliable spreading groundcover or cascading planter perennial.

MAGNOLIA GRANDIFLORA

Also called: *Southern Magnolia*

The magnificent Southern Magnolia is the classic American evergreen tree and a staple in Southern gardens and landscapes for generations. Its grand stature and large waxy white flowers are the very symbol of the South. The scent of the Magnolia Grandiflora flower is sweeter than tea, and its May flowering time is a sure sign that summer's on its way.

The Southern Magnolia is a classic Southern motif on everything from book covers to throw pillows. Its large leathery leaves and distinctly shaped cones are gathered for arts and craft projects, as well as Christmas decorations.

The Magnolia Grandiflora is grown as far north as Cincinnati, Ohio, but begins to disappear further north. It is what botanists call a subtropical indicator, a tree that divides Southern and northern climate zones. One of the Southern Magnolias greatest attributes is the strength of its limbs. It is able to withstand wind and ice storms with its branches intact, therefore able to flower and reproduce again another year. The Southern Magnolia is the largest tree in the Magnolia family, but it is a large family and has many members such as the Star Magnolia, Saucer Magnolia and the Sweet Bay Magnolia. The genus is named after French botanist Pierre Magnol.

MAGNOLIA LILIIFLORA

Also called: *Japanese Magnolia or Tulip Magnolia*

The Japanese Magnolia is not native to Japan, as the name would suggest, but rather to China. The Japanese Magnolia was given to Japan by China centuries ago and both countries have been cultivating it for years. It is now widely planted as an ornamental shrub, or small tree, across the Northern Hemisphere.

The Tulip Magnolia is known to most American gardeners for its early spring flowers that come out before the leaves. The flowers are strongly upright with tightly held petals. The name Tulip Magnolia comes from the fact that its flowers resemble those of the perennial Tulip. The Tulip Magnolia's flower color ranges from light pink to a deep magenta. It is one of the most prolific flowering shrubs in the spring. Many hybrids have been developed, and the modern gardener has many varieties to choose from.

As the flowers fall away and the leaves emerge in late spring, the Tulip Magnolia develops into a magnificent full-bodied shrub. It is a close relative of the classic Southern Magnolia, but is quite different in a number of ways. Smaller in overall size than the Southern Magnolia, Tulip Magnolia is a better choice for the urban gardener with limited space.

MAGNOLIA VIRGINIANA

Also called: *Sweetbay Magnolia*

Sweetbay Magnolia is a shrub variety of Magnolia. Like its cousin, the Southern Magnolia, the Sweetbay is native to Southeastern United States and produces large fragrant white flowers. Unlike the Southern Magnolia, the Sweetbay Magnolia is small and deciduous.

MAHONIA

Also called: *Leather Leafed Mahonia or Oregon Grape*

Mahonia is native to China, but has become a staple in Southern gardens in recent years. It is an upright shade-loving evergreen with medium sized Holly like leaves. The leaves are tough and glaucous, hence the name Leather leaf. The genus Mahonia was named for Bernard McMahon, a nineteenth century American horticulturist from Philadelphia.

The flowers of the Mahonia are a deep rich yellow rosette that sits on top of a whirl of spiky leaves. The flowers emerge in mid spring and, after pollination, give way to drooping clusters of grape bunch like drupes that hang down in four to five inch clusters. The fruit has an outer coating of a gritty waxy substance called bloom. Bloom can also be found on actual grapes (Vitis Rotundifolia). The term bloom, botanically speaking, refers only to this substance and is often incorrectly applied to the blossoming of a flower. In other words, flowers do not bloom — they blossom.

Mahonia is associated with strength, vigor, and defense in lore. It is said to be the last defense against the invasion of regret and is therefore planted when one needs to overcome a torn relationship. Mahonia is a shade-loving plant, and therefore it is known to keep secrets. Its seeds also germinate readily on their own with no pre-treatment, and so the Mahonia has become a symbol of unconditional love.

MALUS

Also called: *Apple or Flowering Crabapple*

Flowering Crabapples are grown by American gardeners mostly for their ornamental value and less as a food source. Crabapples are small to medium sized trees that bare small clusters of white to pink flowers in the spring. They are a perfect way to bring color, structure and butterflies to a small garden or courtyard. Flowering Crabapples are well suited for the urban landscape, as they provide spring flowers, varying leaf color in the summer and fall color that few other small trees can match. Crabapples are in the Rose family and closer inspection of the flower reveals the genealogy.

The Flowering Crabapple fruit begins to develop in late spring and into summer. The small, usually red, fruit is great for attracting birds. This tree is a native of the Northern hemisphere and has been heavily hybridized and planted over the years. Because of the many cultivars, landscapers have many colors and features to chose from. They are insect pollinated, so no insecticide should ever be used on a Crabapple.

The Apple was highly regarded by the Greeks and the Romans. One Mediterranean mythological story tells how Atlanta lost her race by stooping to pick up an Apple that had been dropped by her competitor in a successful attempt to slow her. Her competitor's life was to be forfeited if he did not reach the goal ahead of Atlanta.

There is also the purely American story of Johnny Appleseed, the pioneer nurseryman and conservationist. Johnny Appleseed was a New Englander who went westward across the middle of America spreading Apple seeds as he went. Although a true person, much legend has grown up around his works.

MISCANTHUS SINENSIS 'ZEBRINUS'

Also called: *Zebra Grass*

One of the larger ornamental grasses in Georgia, Zebra Grass is planted for its unique horizontal striped variegation. This fully upright Grass is usually planted as an accent specimen or structure plant in the landscape. It is surpassed in overall size only by Pampas Grass.

Gardeners tend to leave Miscanthus Grasses alone well into winter, as the light beige winter colored foliage and lush plumes are a desirable feature along with the Stripping. Like all ornamental grasses, Zebra Grass needs to be cut down to the ground in the early spring before the new growth begins.

MONARDA

Also called: *Bee Balm*

MUHLENBERGIA

Also called: *Sweetgrass*

Muhlenbergia, or Sweetgrass as most Southerners call it, is a species of ornamental grass. It is native to the Southeastern United States.

Sweetgrass has historical importance in coastal South Carolina, where it has been used for over two hundred years to weave coil baskets. African Americans from the Gullah tradition still weave artistic baskets using this native grass. These museum quality baskets are known in the South Carolina Lowcountry as Sweetgrass baskets.

Outside of South Carolina most landscapers use Sweetgrass as an ornamental grass. Its mounds of soft flowing blades and light purple plume provide texture variations to the mid South garden.

Long a favorite of American gardeners, Monarda is an insouciant perennial for the North Georgia garden. This Mint family member is a North American native that thrives in full sun to part shade with regular water.

The flower of the Monarda sits up on a two or three-foot tall spike and radiates a torch like red flame of color. The flowers are arranged singly on each stalk, but the stalks often grow in groups giving the appearance of a bright red bouquet that lasts all summer. The common name refers to the fact that the flower attracts bees that are necessary for pollination.

Many years ago in a farmhouse on the outskirts of LaGrange, an old peasant sat on his porch watching the sunset. He was just about to get up to go back inside when a figure appeared at the road and seemed to make its way toward the house. The surprised peasant blinked as the meandering man came up to the porch, introduced himself, and said that he was thirsty. He asked for a cup of water, and the old man kindly obliged.

After drinking the water, the visitor asked the ailing old man if he was all right, if he felt well. "Nope," was the old man's reply, "long past help." The visitor said to him, "Do as I bid you now, and you shall again have all of the strength and vigor of a man of twenty years." The visitor continued, "Plant in your garden the flower of the balm of fire, the one called bee. When the balm blossoms red, hold it to your chest and you shall feel your heart beat strong again." Sensing that the visitor's story was true, the old man turned to thank him, but no one was there.

As the autumn leaves fell in swirls of gold and yellow around his head, the man planted Bee Balm in his garden, and hope in his soul. The next summer, when the Bee Balm blossomed, the old man did indeed feel as he had in his youth. The balm of kindness and concern had acted as a salve, for the only ailment that the old man had had was loneliness.

$\mathcal{M}$YRIOPHYLLUM AQUATICUM

Also called: *Parrot's Feather*

Parrot's Feather is a beautiful, fun, and dangerous aquatic plant. Its wispy feathery whorls form dense colonies on the surface of any fresh water source it gets into. While many water gardeners love it for its waving, flowing motion and ease of care, they should be aware of its potential to get out of hand. Parrot's feather is a noxious weed. It is super invasive, immune to most herbicides and actually perpetuated by manual cutting. The smallest fragment of Parrot's feather will root and clog drains and municipal waterways. It will quickly crowd out other aquatic plants and destroy an otherwise balanced ecosystem.

This lacey textured plant also provides a safe habitat for Mosquitoes, therefore promoting Mosquito borne diseases. For these reasons, it is illegal to sell or transport it in many areas.

Parrot's feather is native to South America, but has become naturalized all over the world.

NANDINA DOMESTICA

Also called: *Nandina or Heavenly Bamboo*

Nandina is a wonderful, if sometimes aggressive, garden shrub. Native to China and Japan, it has been planted in America for nearly as long as anyone can remember. Despite the common name Heavenly Bamboo, Nandina is not a Bamboo at all.

Nandina has trifoliate leaves vaguely resembling those of Coral bean. The leaves come in colors ranging from shades of red to lime green at any time of year, with red to orange berries in the fall and into winter. Nandina can grow to over six feet high, and is strongly upright. A nearly carefree plant, it can live for years in full sun or shade.

NICOTIANA ALATA

Also called: *Jasmine Tobacco or Winged Tobacco*

Winged Tobacco is a summer annual bedding or container flower for the North Georgia gardener. It is sometimes called Jasmine Tobacco for its flowers resemblance to Jasmine. Gardeners have a wide range of colors to chose from, everything from white to pink all the way to dark red. Pastel shades are also common among Winged Tobacco.

The botanical name Alata comes from the Latin word for 'winged.'

Nicotiana Alata is in the Solanaceae or Nightshade family, making it related to Petunia, Mandrake, Chili Pepper, Paprika, Potatoes, Tomatoes, and Eggplant, as well as Cigarette Tobacco.

Solanaceae is one of the most important plant families to the study of Ethnobotany. Ethnobotany is the study of the relationship between man and plants. Ethnobotanical fields of study can include cultural, medicinal, culinary, and agricultural studies.

ONOPORDUM

Also called: *Thistle or Scotch Thistle*

It was in the year 1262 that King Alexander the Second of Scotland got tired of the Viking raids that kept happening off the west coast of Scotland. He posted his soldiers at the many castles that dot the landscape. It wasn't long before, at the Castle Largs, that the Vikings raided under the cover of night, thinking that the darkness would obscure their approach. The Vikings wore only sandals, or went barefoot, and we're not expecting a Thistle thicket around the mote of the castle. They yelped in pain as they stepped into the thicket, alerting the Scottish sentries. The sentries then rose up and defended the castle and saved the sovereignty of Scotland. This is one story of how the Thistle became the official emblem of Scotland.

The vegetable known today as Artichoke is actually an unopened Thistle flower bud.

There was once a Thistle gardener who had all sorts of thistles — big ones, small ones, purple ones, and brown ones. This gardener would order Thistle seeds from all over the world. He nearly drove his neighbors mad as they too had a Thistle garden, although a lot less desired. The neighbors got together to devise a plan to get the gardener to stop growing Thistles. At first they offered him shrubs and flowers to replace his thistles, but this did not work. Then, they offered to take him out to get him away from the Thistles, but, alas, every time they made an offer his reply was "No, I can't, I'm stuck in the garden."

OSMANTHUS HETEROPHYLLUS

Also called: *Variegated Osmanthus or Variegated False Holly*

Variegated False Holly is a reliable variegated evergreen shrub that strongly resembles a Holly. With only a few true Hollies providing variegation, Variegated False Holly gives a landscape designer more options and flexibility.

Variegated Osmanthus is a slow growing member of the Olive family Oleaceae. It does not flower profusely and is used mainly as a structure or texture evergreen. Like all plants that are variegated, in time, it will revert back to its natural all green form. It takes a Variegated Osmanthus several years to revert. An unpruned Osmanthus will eventually flower white, but if it is pruned it will produce only vegetative growth.

Also called: *Shamrock or Clover*

While most gardeners consider Oxalis to be a weed, others consider it a welcome flowering plant in the garden. Its small purple to lavender flower is attractive enough, but its leaves are the real desirable feature. Most Shamrock bear three leaves per stem, but one in about ten thousand bear four leaves. For centuries, the Irish have considered this fourth leaf to bring luck to the finder. And so, in modern America it is considered lucky to come upon a four leafed clover.

PACHYSANDRA

Also called: *Spurge or Joy of the Ground*

Spurge is a Japanese groundcover plant for shady areas. Chinese herbalists believed that this evergreen ground plant could be gathered only on the first, ninth, eleventh, or thirteenth day of the Moon by a person cleansed of all impurities.

In middle eastern areas it was believed that whoever carried the Spurge was protected from evil spirits and safe from the bites of rabid dogs and venomous spiders.

The Scots named this powerful plant Joy of the Ground. They believed that marital bliss would be ensured if the plants were planted around the house and eaten at meals.

PAEONIACEAE

Also called: Peony or May Flower

The Peony is an Atlanta garden favorite and one of its most reliable perennials. The Peony has become an old fashioned flowering plant here in America and is well suited to Atlanta's hot summers and cool winters. It flowers exclusively in May, hence the name May Flower. There are many varieties and colors of Peonies to choose from. Peonies have three main types of flowers; single, double and full, also known as "Peony style." Peonies are originally native to China.

A Chinese botanist spent his life caring for the Peony plant. He had spent so many years in the company of the Peony that he had no friends or family left, as time went on, he became in need of an employee to help him care for his growing collection of flowers.

As luck would have it, a beautiful young girl knocked on his door and asked if she could work for him. The botanist was happy to employ her and teach her the ways of the Peony. She was, as it turned out, a perfect student. The girl was quick to learn, of impeccable character, morally honorable and dedicated to both the botanist and the Peony collection.

One day, a long-lost love of the botanist's came to the door for a visit. Wanting to introduce the woman to the young pupil, the botanist called to the student, and when she did not answer, went looking for her, but could not find her. He went into the greenhouse to search for her and found her flat against the wall hiding behind a piece of glass. No longer in human form, but now a painting, the young girl said to the botanist, "I did not answer you for I am no longer human, but have become the soul of the Peony." The girl in the painting continued, "Your love warmed me into a human and it has been my joy to serve you, but you now have a real human to love and you no longer need me. Enjoy me as a flower, care for me as your own, but go and love her with all your heart." As the moments passed, the botanist's heart both broke and grew. He returned to his door. With tears of sadness and joy he invited the woman in. The botanist knew when the woman said, "I love you. I've missed you terribly and I'm glad to be back with you and your beautiful Peony collection" that the young girl was right to return to the flowers.

Also called: _Princess or Empress Tree_

The common name Princess Tree, as well as the genus, was named in honor of Anna Paulownia of Russia, princess of the Netherlands. Other common names for Paulownia include Empress Tree and Royal Paulownia. The Chinese valued it for its ornamental beauty as well as for its high quality lumber.

An old tradition, in China, is to plant the Empress Tree when a baby girl is born. The tradition says that the tree matures as she does. When she has matured to an age where she is eligible for marriage, the tree is carved into wooden items for her dowry.

Carving the wood of the Paulownia is an art form in China and Japan, and has been for centuries. In legend, it is said that the mythical Phoenix will only land on the Empress Tree, and only when a perfect emperor is in power. Also, several string instruments are made from the Paulownia, among them are the Japanese Koto and the Korean Gayageum zithers. The wood can also be made into chests, boxes and other household goods.

In the United States, a wash was made from the leaves to bathe sore and tender feet. The inner bark, soaked in whiskey, was used to treat fevers. Liver ailments were often treated with a mixture of Princess Tree flowers and other herbs. A liquid, obtained by crushing the leaves, was used to get rid of warts. Today, the lightweight wood is made into furniture, and other specialty items, such as footwear.

The flowers of the Paulownia are noted for their strong resemblance to the perennial Foxglove (Digitalis). They are in large elongated clusters and borne along the massive branches that can be up to twenty-five feet long. The Empress Tree is also noteworthy for its enormous leaves that resemble the Southern Catalpa. This tree can reach heights of over fifty feet.

PERILLA FRUTESCENS

Also called: *Purple Perilla, Wild Mint Basil, or Rattlesnake Mint*

Perilla is a self-seeding annual herb native to Asia. It is in the Mint family. It is also a traditional medicinal and culinary herb in China, Japan, Korea, India, and Thailand. Spice traders brought Perilla to the United States in the late nineteenth century, and it has quickly naturalized and become a common self-seeding annual in pastures and gardens in the Southeastern United States. Though it can be found in cultivation and available for sale, most gardeners treat it as a wildflower. Therefore it is often traded by neighbors or at plant swaps.

Perilla can be found growing in sunny open fields, riparian areas, and semi-shady woodlands. Perilla prefers slightly moist well-drained soil in full sun, but will grow in partial shade. It is a desirable plant for the garden, as it attracts butterflies and can add a hue of purple that is otherwise rare. Although it is technically an annual, it will spread on its own by seed, but it is not invasive. It's dark purple stems and purple to red hued leaves last all summer and into the fall. It is a somewhat aromatic plant, with a mild minty smell. Growing to over three feet tall by the end of the growing season, the branching stems are square, and reddish purple.

The leaves are large — up to five inches in diameter — with wavy margins. They are opposite, ovate and serrate, dark green tinted red to purple and hairy. The flower spikes are long, up to ten inches and borne in the leaf axils. The numerous flowers are small and tubular, pink to lavender. After blooming from July to October, they leave their calyx on the spike to cover the seedpod. Shake the dry seed stalks and it sounds like a rattlesnake. That's how the plant got one of its common names, Rattlesnake Mint.

Perilla is ideal for both medicinal and culinary uses. There are many unproven medicinal uses for Perilla that should be taken as lore. It has been used for centuries in Oriental medicine as an antiasthmatic, antibacterial, antiseptic, aromatic, expectorant, and tonic. An infusion of Perilla is useful in the treatment of asthma, colds, cough and lung afflictions, and to restore health and wellness. The stems and branches are a traditional Chinese remedy for morning sickness during pregnancy.

The leaves have a pleasant sweet taste and are used as a spice-cooking herb combined with fish, rice, vegetables, and soups. It can also be added to stir-fries and salads. It can be used as a Basil substitute. Cooking oil is derived from the seed, as well as giving color and flavor to many pickled dishes. In the United States the essential oil of the plant is used as a food flavoring in candies and sauces. The entire plant is very nutritious, packed with vitamins and minerals.

Perilla seed oil has been used in paints, varnishes, linoleum, printing inks, lacquers, and as waterproof coatings on cloth. Natural oils of the plant are also used in aromatherapy and for perfume. Burning dried Perilla produces potent incense. The seed heads can be collected and dried for use in floral arrangements, herbal potpourris, and wreaths. The crushed plant also makes an effective insecticide.

For centuries, religious ceremonies were conducted before harvesting the plant. It was considered to be alive and was thought to be sacred, sent by the spirits to provide food and medicine for mankind. Disrespect for the plant meant death, and anyone who stepped on the plant would himself be trampled to death. At the end of the winter, the dried arrangements were burned with the expectation that the smoke would arouse the sleeping gods and prompt them to bring the Perilla back again for another season.

PHILADELPHUS

Also called: *Mock Orange*

The Mock Orange is a beautiful ornamental shrub that provides both pristine white flowers and a sweet scent to the Georgia garden. The Mock Orange's white cross-shaped flowers are framed by lush soft green leaves on stout upright stems. The Philadelphus flower blossoms in the later part of spring, usually in mid-May. The scent of the Mock Orange is reminiscent of the unrelated Citrus plant, hence the common name.

The Mock Orange has many family members that are familiar to the Southern gardener; among them are the Deutzia, Hydrangea, Tree Anemone, Decumaria, and the Lilac.

$\mathcal{P}$HYSOSTEGIA VIRGINIANA

Also called: *Obedient Plant or False Dragonhead*

The Obedient Plant is a fun and unique native perennial. It gets its common name, Obedient Plant, because of its flowers willingness to stay in place when moved manually. This attribute is unique to the Physostegia genus.

Obedient Plant is a colony forming upright garden flower. It is insect pollinated and therefore attracts butterflies and moths, as well as bees. The fall blossoming flowers are borne in whirls on stout square stems that can reach up to three feet tall. Lush green foliage adorns the Obedient Plant in the spring and summer months. The purple, lavender or white flowers are trumpet shaped with a fluted opening somewhat reminiscent of a miniature Foxglove (Digitalis). The flowers blossom from September to November in the Atlanta area, but flower into December or January in Macon. Obedient Plant can be grown in the shade or in full sun and makes an excellent cut flower. It is a member of the Mint family.

The False Dragonhead can be an aggressive spreader, especially in moist conditions; it will also spread by rhizomes in drier conditions, but with far less vigor. It will quickly form colonies, so give it room to form a mass planting. It is best to plant it in a relatively dry or well-drained area, and plan to divide it occasionally. False Dragonhead should never need fertilizer. Despite these warnings, Physostegia Virginiana is a beautiful flowering plant when viewed in mass colonies.

℘ICEA PUNGENS 'GLAUCA GLOBOSA'

Also called: Globe Blue Spruce or Dwarf Colorado Blue Spruce

There is much folklore about the Spruce tree, one such mythological story comes from the Haida native Indian tradition.

The legend relates that two sisters who were being treated cruelly by their stepmother decided to leave their home. Sometime later they were found by a kind man who took them in and married them. After some years they decided to revisit their childhood homeland, but this meant a journey of some difficulty and distance. The good spirits of the Spruce bade them weave two baskets apiece from Spruce tips, small enough to fit over the ends of their thumbs. These they were to fill with dried meat and Chaste berries. Now these little baskets, holding less than a mouthful apiece, were as the baskets that contained the loaves and fishes, for though the two sisters ate all they wished, the supply of food never diminished. When they arrived at their stepmothers lodge, the baskets suddenly swelled to the size they would have reached had they contained the food actually used on the journey. The old stepmother was still there, and, being easily persuaded to eat of the contents of the baskets, gorged to such a degree that she could no longer breathe. She died in a rapture of gluttonous bliss, and the stepdaughters were avenged.

The Dwarf Colorado Blue Spruce is a hybrid, developed for the landscape trade. It has many of the characteristics of one of its parent plants, the famous Colorado blue spruce, but is very different in shape and size. Dwarf Colorado blue spruce is short, round, and compact. It is a perfect size for the urban landscape and adds evergreen color to the winter garden. It is highly valued as an ornamental conifer for its silver green needles that contrast well with other foliage. The Atlanta area is on the southern end of the globe's Blue Spruce's range, preferring a northern slope exposure and some protection from the summer sun. There are many Piceas from which to choose, everything from globe shaped to fully upright. Be careful not to water a Picea in the winter months, as the roots prefer to be on the dry side.

Pieris Japonica is a somewhat floppy, drooping evergreen shrub. It shows beautiful fall color from the first hint of colder weather through the winter. In the spring, Pieris Japonica produces a profusion of small bell like flowers that cascade down the side of arching branches. Pieris is a semi-shade plant needing to be sheltered from the harshest afternoon sun. Most varieties are three to four feet tall, but a couple varieties are over six feet. Japanese Andromeda needs plenty of water until it is established in the garden.

Once it is a year or so old, it is a nearly maintenance-free shrub, needing only to be deadheaded in early August.

Pieris Japonica gets its common name, Japanese Andromeda, from the constellation and galaxy Andromeda. Andromeda is an astrological constellation in the Northern sky that was named for the princess from the Greek mythological story of Perseus. Ancient Japanese emperors thought that the flowers of the Pieris looked like, and therefore named it after, the astrological constellation and galaxy.

*P*LATANUS OCCIDENTALIS

Also called: *Sycamore or Buttonwood Tree*

On May 17, 1792, twenty-four stock brokers got together on Wall Street in Manhattan, under a Buttonwood tree, to sign what would become known as "The Buttonwood Agreement." The Buttonwood agreement, in short, cut out the auctioneers and set certain rates and percentages. These papers, named for the tree under which they were signed, were the founding documents for what we know today as The New York Stock Exchange.

The New York Stock Exchange would not exist had it not been for "The Buttonwood Agreement."

While Buttonwood is a common name for Platanus Occidentalis, most know it simply as the Sycamore tree. The Sycamore tree is one of the most ubiquitous deciduous hardwood trees in North America, growing from Canada to Florida. The Sycamore's most widely recognizable feature is its bark. The exfoliating bark peels off in pale gray plates, showing large areas of its smooth white trunk and branches. A massive tree, the Sycamore can get to well over eighty feet tall and wide. The leaves of the Buttonwood are also noteworthy for their size, being among the largest in the deciduous forest.

PLATYCODON GRANDIFLORUS

Also called: *Japanese Bellflower or Balloon Flower*

Balloon Flower gets its common name because its flower bud puffs up like a balloon before opening into an upward facing, bell shaped flower with five pointed lobes. A single Bellflower has only one petal that is complete around the stamen set. Balloon Flower is a low clump forming perennial for the full sun to part shade garden. North Georgia gardeners like Balloon Flowers for their ease of care. They need only be watered a few times after planting for years of color in the border.

A small plant overall, Balloon Flower's come in several colors, including blue, purple and white. Several varieties of Balloon Flowers are variegated, with swirls of opposing colors on the petal. The Bellflower is in the Campanula family and is native to China, Japan and Korea.

Platycodon has a long history as an herbal medicine in Japan and Korea. The root of the Platycodon has been used traditionally for its anti-inflammatory qualities. Its flower is also used as a symbol by several cities and institutions.

PLUMBAGO

Also called: *Leadwort*

A sprawling but reliable plant, Plumbago is a tender dieback shrub or annual in North Georgia. Any frost bitten growth will need to be cut to the ground in early spring, but it does flower on new growth, so the North Georgia gardener can enjoy flowers each year. Gardeners closer to Augusta and Macon will generally have more success with Plumbago than gardeners in Rome or the mountains. The abundant flowers are five-petaled and come in colors ranging from white to orange red. Plumbago needs full sun and plenty of water. Lime must not be added to the soil around the Plumbago, as it needs more acidic conditions.

Plumbago is a sprawling shrub that, left untrimmed, will scamper up larger trees or other structures. If assiduously pruned, the Plumbago can be neat in form and overall texture. It is without thorns and is safe to have around decks or patios that are used during the summer months.

The other common name, Leadwort, dates back to the time of Pliny the Elder. Pliny the Elder was a Roman naturalist who lived in the first century CE and was one of the first to document nature. He thought that the flower of the Plumbago had the hue of lead and therefore referred to it as Leadwort.

Portulaca Grandiflora

Also called: *Moss Rose*

Moss Rose is a heat loving summer annual in the American garden. Portulaca is well suited to hot, dry sunny weather. It is one of only a few succulent annuals. Many gardeners plant this sun lover for its bright, cheerful colors that come in a kaleidoscope of hues and configurations. There are many types and mixes of Moss Rose available for the Southern flower enthusiast.

In its native Brazil, Portulaca is considered by tribesmen to be one of the flowers of the sun gods. While many other flowers shy away from the brutal Brazilian sun, Portulaca worshiped the sun and thrived. Over the years, the Brazilian tribes began to worship the Portulaca for its ability to survive the harsh sun and dry conditions, hoping that the Portulaca might carry their favor to the sun gods.

PRIMULA

Also called: *Primrose*

Primrose: an original poem

Primrose, Primrose in swirls of motley
of the English countryside, you do remind me
at Hampton Court Palace, the flower show
in six neat rows, for the sun's own glory
just beyond where the Monkey Puzzle grows
Primrose, Primrose worth the crime
after Primrose, there is only time
In the hope of Primrose, and an imperfect sage
the wildest of flowers ensnare no less than the Queen
the Primrose shall flower, and so shall her suitor
I know who I am now, I am a gardener
tending the earth, where no yellow Roses grow
Lest we forget the wood house and her calling
flowers don't speak, but only in volumes

*P*RUNUS

Also called: *Cherry*

Prunus trees are planted for their ornamental spring blossoms. Despite their name, they do not produce cherries. This Japanese native tree is strictly an ornamental, but is still a popular lawn tree.

*P*YRACANTHA KOIDZUMII

Also called: *Pyracantha or Firethorn*

Firethorn is an evergreen shrub native to Southern Asia. Pyracantha gets the common name Firethorn for its large thorns and for the fire red berries that develop in the fall in clusters at the tips of the branches. Firethorn has small white flowers in the spring that develop in to the fruits. Although it is a shrub, Firethorn has the structure of a vine. Its branches sprawl out in irregular patterns to lengths of fifteen feet or more.

In the United States, Pyracantha is grown as an ornamental espalier. They are most often trained against a wall for support, but are occasionally grown as a freestanding Shrub. Pyracantha is a tough plant that grows well in full sun or heavy shade. It attracts all manner of wildlife, and should be planted in any wildlife garden. Pyracantha is hardy from the southern parts of Illinois and Indiana south to Florida.

Of all the trees in ancient history, the Oak was the most widely venerated of the sacred plants because in the mythological belief of many tribes and clans, it was the first tree to exist and man was created from it.

In antiquity, the Oak tree became sacred to the Hebrews when Abraham received an Angel of Jehovah under its branches. The Greeks dedicated the Oak to Zeus because his oracle was in the ancient town of Dodona, which was located in a grove of Oaks. To the Romans, the Oak was the tree of Jupiter.

While mythological and historical stories about the Oak tree reach as far back as storytelling itself, the Willow Oak specifically is native to the Southeastern United States. A tall, wide and fairly uniform tree, the Willow Oak is an Atlanta gardeners' best choice for quick shade and beautiful yellow fall color. The botanical name "Phellos" comes from the Greek word "Philo," meaning brotherly love; the common name "Willow" refers to the leaves resemblance to those of the Salix, or Willow family.

QUERCUS RUBRA

Also called: *Red Oak*

Red Oaks are large shade trees that are most often planted for their fall color. Red Oaks differ from white Oaks in one distinct way: the lobes of their leaves are sharp and pointed.

RAPHIOLEPIS

Also called: *Majestic Beauty or Indian Hawthorn*

Majestic Beauty is a large evergreen shrub grown for its large clusters of pink flowers.

RHODODENDRON PENTANTHERA

Also called: *Native Azalea*

There are many gardeners beginning to go natural. These organic gardeners are turning off their sprinkler systems and using compost instead of chemical fertilizers, with better results. Natural gardeners are beginning to seek out native plants — plants that were growing in their area before Europeans arrived and are well adapted to that climate.

The Azalea, a traditional Southern shrub, is known for its early spring flowers that wake up a Georgia garden from its winter slumber. While most Azaleas are native to Asia, there are a number of Azaleas that are native to the Eastern United States. These Azaleas often flower early in the year, before the leaves emerge, with a distinctive trumpet like flower. The botanical name Pentanthera refers to the penta, or five, anthers of the flower. Native Azaleas tend to be long flowering, deciduous, upright and come in warm colors ranging from yellow and pink to orange. In North Georgia they are nearly maintenance free, provided they have some afternoon shade. Many of the native Rhododendron Pentanthera species also flower again in the autumn. Native Azalea species that can be seen in Atlanta and the surrounding areas include: R. Atlanticum, R. Canadense, R. Arborescens, and R. Viscosum.

Native Azaleas attract a wide variety of wildlife; including butterflies, moths, birds, and squirrels.

ROSA LAEVIGATA

Also called: *Cherokee Rose or Rose Camellia*

The Cherokee Rose is a scandent evergreen vine-like climber and a true member of the Rose family. The Cherokee Rose is the state flower of Georgia. It was adopted by the state legislature in 1916.

Although native to Southeast Asia, from China to Taiwan, the Cherokee Rose has naturalized in the Southern United States. It is an easy plant to care for, requiring only occasional pruning. Differing from hybrid Roses, the Cherokee Rose is not bothered by insects or fungi. The white flower of the Rosa Laevigata has a single petal arrangement with a gold stamen set, strongly resembling a Camellia.

Thomas Jefferson wrote in his journal for April 29, 1804: "Planted seeds of the Cherokee rose from Gov. Milledge (John Milledge of Georgia) in a row of about 6 f. near the N.E. corner of the nursery. Goliah stuck sticks to mark the place." Goliah was the head gardener at Monticello, Jefferson's home.

SALVIA LEUCANTHA

Also called: *Mexican Sage*

A mounding, mostly upright perennial, Mexican Sage is a beautiful and unique flower for the late summer garden. It is a sun-loving member of the Sage family that develops fuzzy blue to purple flowers in late August and into September. Flowers of the Mexican Sage are insect pollinated and insecticides will harm the reproduction and flowering process. The flowers sit up on slender arching stems above neat mounds of silver green lanceolate leaves that are themselves furry on the undersides.

Salvia Leucantha is native to Mexico and Central America. The book *Savannah's* *Garden Plants* contains a story about the flower Ruellia, or Mary's Flower. That story tells of how the Ruellia is cut to bring into Catholic Cathedrals as an offering to the Virgin Mary, the mother of Jesus. The Ruellia is a summer flowering plant that grows wild in the same general areas as the Mexican Sage. When the Ruellia stops flowering in the late summer, Mexican Catholics begin to pick the purple flowers of the Mexican Sage, so into the fall they can continue to have a royal purple flower to offer to the Virgin Mary.

SAMBUCUS

Also called: *Elderberry or Common Elder*

Lurking in shadowy under stories and dark forests, the Elderberry came to be regarded as having supernatural associations. In Northern Europe it was said to be possessed of a spirit, and no one could destroy it without peril to himself.

Its name associates it with Hulda, or Hilda, mother of elves, the good woman in Northern myths. In Denmark, Hulda lived in the root of the Elder, hence the shrub was her symbol, and was used during the ritual ceremonies of her worship.

It was forbidden to use Elderberry wood in the construction of houses. It was said that the occupant of such a house would feel the pulling of the spirits in his legs, a nasty sensation that could only be relieved by planting three Elderberry shrubs in the forest and assuring their life until maturity and flowering.

Incidentally, Elder wood cures toothaches and fends off snakes, mosquitoes, and warts. It quiets nerves and interrupts fits of madness, removes poison from metal pitchers, keeps fleas out of furniture, makes the home safe and guarantees he who cultivates it shall die in his own house. While the large white Elderberry flowers were said to represent the purity and brightness of enlightenment, its black berries were gobbled up by all manner of nymphs, fairies, trolls and warlocks.

Despite all these wonderfully enchanting myths from Europe, Elderberry is also native to the Eastern United States, making it a valuable addition to any native garden. As a large flowering shrub, Elderberry is a standout among its peers. Elderberry wine has long been a traditional drink in many cultures.

SELAGINELLA

Also called: *Spike Moss or Peacock Feather Moss*

This fun and easy to grow plant is a favorite with outdoor gardeners and terrarium keepers alike. Not a true Moss, Spike Moss is a very versatile plant provided it is kept moist and in a shady spot. Spike Moss is a low growing spreading Fern like plant that is usually seen growing over shady border beds or up against old growth trees. Selaginella is a texture plant that does not flower. It can easily be divided and put directly into moist soil in a pot or in the ground, and is therefore a great choice for children's gardening projects.

Selaginella, as a family, can be found growing all over the world. A diverse family, they range from bog to desert plants.

$\mathcal{S}$ENECIO CINERARIA

Also called: *Dusty Miller*

What's in a name? Well, in the case of Dusty Miller, a lot of confusion. No less than eight different garden plants share the common name Dusty Miller. All of the plants with the common name Dusty Miller share some similar character traits: they all have silvery grey, felt like foliage, they are all mounding sun lovers and they all flower yellow. This is a good lesson in the importance of botanical names. There is only one garden plant known as Senecio Cineraria, the most common Dusty Miller.

Dusty Miller is a low growing member of the Aster family that likes full sun. While it does flower, most gardeners grow Dusty Miller for its fury silver foliage. Pinching out the developing flowers in the center of the mound helps the Dusty Miller to grow fuller. The Senecio Cineraria likes cool wet winters and hot dry summers. In the north Georgia area it is considered a somewhat reliable perennial.

A Miller, by trade, is one who mills or grinds to produce a product. The Dusty Miller gets its common name from the earth spirits who live under the leaves of the Senecio. In Mediterranean lore, the dust spirits would mill or grind fairy dust to spread magic around the land. Any plant that was covered in the miller's dust would then have magical powers. Dusty Miller henceforth became an important ingredient in magical potions.

In another version of the same tale, Dusty Miller could be magically turned into silver. It was said that if the silver was used for pious and right purposes, the user would find good luck, but if the user turned the Dusty Miller to silver for nefarious purposes, the act would turn back on him.

$\mathcal{S}$OLENOSTEMON

Also called: *Coleus*

A popular garden plant, Coleus is grown for its amazing foliage color and texture patterns. In the North Georgia area Coleus is grown as an annual, while in southern Georgia it is a tender herbaceous perennial. The North Georgia gardener can simply cut Coleus sections in the fall and put them in a glass of room temperature water or pot them to root over the winter months. They can then be planted outside after the danger of frost has passed. In this respect, Coleus is an evergreen, living half a year as a garden plant and half a year as a houseplant.

Coleus comes in a wide variety of colors that are matte in finish and almost always brightly displayed. The color patterns vary wildly, even among plants in the same genus. While Coleus does flower, it is grown as a foliage plant. The main attraction of the Coleus is its color, but the various foliage shapes and styles have not been lost on gardeners looking for texture or structure in the summer garden. A Coleus can have a smooth or serrated margin, that same margin can be flat or wavy. The possibilities are nearly endless. Although it can be grown in full sun when watered well, Coleus will have brighter colors and less maintenance when grown in part shade or dappled sunlight. Coleus is in the Mint family and is native to tropical Africa, Asia and Australia.

The common name Coleus comes from the now discontinued genus name Coleus, that itself comes from the Greek word koleos, meaning sheath. The male portions of Coleus flowers, the stamens, are fused into a tube or sheath. The botanical name Solenostemon comes from the Latin word Sol, meaning Sun. The botanical name also contains the word stem or on a stem, with the whole word meaning "Held up on a stem to the Sun." The word Sol has also led to this plant's association with the Roman sun god Sol.

Also called: *Goldenrod*

Goldenrod is America's native wildflower. It is one of North Americas most widely spread wildflowers and can be seen along roads and across fields from Northern Ontario to Florida. It is named Goldenrod for the profusion of yellow flowers that grace the top of three-foot long stems. Goldenrod is the state flower of Kentucky, where it was adopted in 1926 and Nebraska, where it was adopted in 1895. In Delaware, Solidago Odora, a type of Goldenrod, is the official state herb.

Solidago has been unfairly blamed for causing hay fever, which it does not. Hay fever is caused by the unrelated Ragweed, which blossoms at the same time. In fact, Solidago has been used in natural medicine practices for centuries.

There are many different types of Goldenrods, but they do all have some characteristics in common. All Goldenrods are insect pollinated perennials with unmistakable bright yellow flowers that emerge in late summer into early fall. Some Goldenrods arch and some are strongly upright. They will form colonies by seed or with new but related plants growing on underground rhizomes.

British gardeners adopted Goldenrod long before Americans. Goldenrod only began to gain some acceptance in American gardening (other than wildflower gardening) during the 1980s. A new Solidago hybrid with Aster, known as X Solidaster is more manageable. It also has pale yellow flowers that are equally suitable for dried arrangements. Solidago Canadensis was introduced as a garden plant in Central Europe, and is now common in the wild.

Goldenrod is a companion plant, hosting some beneficial insects, and repelling some pests.

$\mathcal{S}$PIREA

Also called: *Meadow Sweet*

Spirea is a medium to large flowering shrub in the Rose family. There are two main types of Spirea: the bridal wreath group and the clumping group. The bridal wreath varieties have small white flowers in abundance along the length of multiple, slender arching stems. The clumping group is much lower and mound forming with pink to salmon flowers that mass at the top of the leaves. All Spireas, regardless of group, have leaves that are small with sharply serrated margins. Spirea leaves can be either blunt or elongated. They are deciduous, and can be cut to the ground in the winter if needed.

Meadow Sweet is also a food source for many kinds of moths, including the Brown-Tail and the Setaceous Hebrew Character.

Aspirin is the generic medical name for the chemical acetylsalicylic acid, a derivative of salicylic acid. Compounds of salicylic acid are found in Spirea. Acetyl and Spirea are the words that inspired the name "aspirin"; yet, despite this connection to aspirin, Spireas are considered to be toxic and should not be used as a pain reliever.

STACHYS

Also called: *Lamb's Ear*

Lamb's Ear is a reliable perennial grown for its grey to silver foliage. The leaves of the Lamb's Ear plant are soft and velvety. The six to seven-inch leaf resembles in many ways that of a Lamb's ear, hence the common name. A tough persistent perennial for the sun or dappled shade, Lamb's Ear adds greatly to the texture of a garden design plan without adversely affecting the color scheme. Although it does produce flowers, most gardeners trim off the flowers to help this plant grow larger leaves. Occasional cleanup is needed to help Lamb's Ear look it's best, but the effort goes a long way in adding to the summer garden.

Beyond its use as an ornamental garden plant, Stachys has been used as a medicinal plant throughout the world for centuries. It is most notable among herbalists for its wound healing properties. Ancient Romans would have called this plant Woundwort and would have considered it a regular part of daily life.

TAGETES

Also called: *Marigold*

An annual flower for the summer color bed, Marigolds are an old fashioned garden classic. The traditional color of the Marigold is a golden orange, but new hybrids have added yellow, red and white to the mix. Marigolds have become a favorite of elementary teachers and a hit with their students. Marigolds are easy to start from seed, need little care and are fast growers. They are a perfect plant for a beginning gardener.

Marigolds are native to the Southwestern United States into Mexico and throughout South America. Explorers first took Marigolds back to Europe in the sixteenth century and gardeners worldwide have been planting them ever since.

$\mathcal{T}$AXODIUM DISTICHUM

Also called: *Swamp Cypress or Bald Cypress*

A native of the Southeastern United states, the Bald Cypress is one of the few conifers in the world that is deciduous. The Bald Cypress is an ornamental tree for most landscapers, although natural stands grow widely across the South.

Native tree lovers and urban gardeners alike grow Bald Cypress for its feathery leaves, uniform structure and russet fall color. It has medium green leaves that are light in texture and wave gently in the slightest wind. The Taxodium is a well-proportioned tree, with a strong central leader and a very conical overall shape. The base of this tree can develop a buttress, which spreads out to provide stability in a swampy location, but this skirting is rarely seen on Bald Cypresses grown in stable soil. The Bald Cypress is a large tree best utilized in landscapes over an acre in size. Like all conifers, it is cone producing; however, the cones of the Bald Cypress are round, greenish grey and tightly formed. The cones are about the size of a golf ball.

The most interesting feature of the Bald Cypress is, however, its knees. The knees are wooden protrusions near the base. They are around two to four feet in height, cylindrical and rounded at the top. Biologist are not sure what their function is exactly, but most agree they are used by the tree to gather more oxygen in a wet location. A Bald Cypress tree grown on solid ground can and will still produce knees, but with much less regularity.

Ancient peoples feared and worshipped the Bald Cypress. In folklore, the god of lightning would strike trees to show his wrath. A tree destroyed and killed by the god of lightning was a warning to the people to obey, but, the Bald Cypress, after being struck by lightning, would re-grow from the roots. The ancient people thought that this meant that the Bald Cypress was more powerful than the god of lightning, and therefore worshipped its regenerative powers. Just to be sure, they also continued to worship the god of lightning.

THUNBERGIA

Also called: *Black Eyed Susan Vine or Clockvine*

Most Southern gardeners know this annual vine as Black Eyed Susan Vine for its strong resemblance to the perennial garden flower Black Eyed Susan. Other gardeners prefer the name Clockvine for its tendency to twine clockwise around objects for support.

Gardeners think of this annual as a safe, un-invasive way to have a scandent vine with flowers for the summertime. Mostly grown from seed, this vine can be seen growing just about anywhere during the summer months. Novice gardeners and flower lovers alike enjoy this vine's medium sized yellow flowers borne in abundance along twenty-foot shoots.

Thunbergias is a close relative of the Greek plant Acanthus. The genus Thunbergia is named for the Swiss botanist, Carl Peter Thunberg, who was also a student's of Carolus Linnaeus.

IBOUCHINA

Also called: Princess Flower or Glory Flower

Glory Flower is a tropical shrub or small tree native to Brazil and parts of Central America. In the Atlanta garden they are considered an annual or a potted plant. Glory flowers cannot stand any frost and will begin to go down when temperatures reach even the mid forties Fahrenheit.

Princess Flowers can bring outstanding color and leaf texture diversity to the Atlanta summer garden. With its large bright flowers and soft velvet leaves, Tibouchina is a great addition to a tropical themed pool or deck area. The greatest attribute of Glory flower is its deep rich purple flower, very rare in the garden color palette.

TILIA CORDATA

Also called: Linden, Lime Tree, or Tree of Myth and Medicine

The Linden tree, as it is most widely known in America, is a durable medium sized street tree in the northern Atlanta area. Linden trees line several streets with its distinctive sweet scented flowers in the spring and pleasing yellow fall color. About the size of a Dogwood in most gardens, the Tilia Cordata tree with its regular branch structure and easy seasonal care is a welcome addition to any neighborhood. Although sometimes called Lime Tree, Tilia Cordatas are not true citrus trees and do not produce citrus limes.

Limes, as they are known in Europe, are a tree of antiquity in England, across France, and into Austria, with many specimens reaching over a thousand years old. There is one Lime tree in Schenklengsfeld, Germany, that is said to have been planted in 760 C.E., making it 1,249 years old. This Lime is known to be among "The Justice Limes," a group of Limes that, in days past, were said to have been where justice was executed.

In European medicinal tradition, an herbal brew was made from the flowers of the Lime tree. Nicholas Culpeper, an English physician from the sixteenth century, noted that Linden flower brew was good for treating dementia, vertigo, and an irregular heartbeat. Some doctors today still think it is useful as a general tonic. Linden flowers are also used in some European beauty products and as a fragrance for skin lotions and potpourris. In France, the Lime was used as a symbol of love and friendship. A sign on the Linden tree in the village of Lucheux, France, known locally as The Lovers Tree, invites newly-wedded couples to walk under it in order to bring many happy years of marriage.

TRACHYCARPUS FORTUNEI

Also called: *Windmill Palm*

The Windmill Palm is cold hardy and will grow well in all of North Georgia. In the most mountainous areas, however, it will need a lot of protection in the winter including a thick layer of mulch. With minimal care beyond covering during cold weather, the Windmill Palm will add a tropical feel to any Georgia landscape.

The Windmill Palm gets its common name from the shape of its fronds, which resemble a rotating windmill. Like all Palms, The Windmill Palm is slow to develop a trunk and will add less than five inches in height a year. They have a much slimmer trunk than most Palms, with the average trunk measuring less than eight inches in diameter. The remaining part of a trimmed frond, on the trunk, is called a boot. The Windmill Palm is native to Southern China, where it has been cultivated for thousands of years.

Many gardeners are familiar with coco liners that are used for flower box frames. The coco liners are made with the hairy material that grows around the trunk of the Trachycarpus Fortunei. Despite the name coco being applied to one of its attributes, the Windmill Palm is not a Coconut Palm and will not produce real coconuts.

TROPAEOLUM

Also called: *Nasturtium*

While many gardeners grow Nasturtiums as a showy annual bedding plant, it has historically been used for salad greens. The whole Nasturtium plant is edible, used as a fresh green or colorful garnish. The flavor of the Nasturtium has been described over the years as everything from peppery to acrid. The circular, trumpet shaped flowers of the Nasturtium range from a bright red to a pale yellow. Many gardeners also note the flat peltate, or round, leaves as a distinguishing feature.

The Nasturtium is a wonderful companion plant in the full sun summer border, planted along with Snapdragons, Poppies, and Sunflowers. Gardeners with an adroit sense of height variations in a garden design often use Nasturtium as the low growing color foundation.

$\int u$ B'Shevat

Also called: *New Year of the Trees*

Tu B'shevat is a minor Jewish holiday. The name Tu B'Shevat comes from the Hebrew name for the date and month in which it is celebrated. Tu B'Shevat means the fifteenth of Shevat. Tu B'Shevat usually falls in late January or early February on the Gregorian calendar and marks the "New Year of the Trees."

Tu B'Shevat is a joyous holiday, the celebration of the planting of trees and harvesting of fruits. A Tu B'Shevat Seder has developed as a festive meal that includes eating dried fruits and nuts, such as Figs, Dates, Raisins, Pomegranates, and Almonds to celebrate the "New Year of the Trees." The Tu B'Shevat Seder also includes readings from Jewish literature about the abundance of the trees and the fruits of the vine. In Israel, the Almond tree flowers around the time of Tu B'shevat, and so has become a symbol of the holiday.

In Jewish law it was forbidden to harvest fruit in the first, second or third year after planting. The fourth year the harvest was to be brought to Jerusalem according to the biblical laws of tithing. The fifth year the fruit could be harvested for culinary and commercial reasons. Since it was impossible to determine the planting date of every tree, a holiday for the birthday of the trees was established. The fifteenth of Shevat was traditionally the date for calculating when the agricultural cycle began or ended.

In modern times, many Israeli environmental groups have adopted the Tu B'Shevat as a day to raise awareness of eco programs. It is also a day that many Jews plant new trees.

For the non-Jewish tree enthusiast, one can think of Tu B'Shevat as a Jewish Arbor day, a day to plant a tree or to reflect on the goodness and benefits of trees.

JULBAGHIA

Also called: *Society Garlic*

Society Garlic gets its common name from the old wives tale that says it can be used in place of garlic at a society gathering, and not cause bad breath.

Society Garlic is a short, Chive like flowering perennial. The fleshy green leaves grow directly from the bulb style rhizome, while the small lavender flowers sit directly on top of the peduncle. The scent of the flower is most notable at night, giving off a sweet fragrance that smells more like a wildflower than like Garlic. Tulbaghia is native to South Africa, but has been grown by European and American gardeners for centuries.

This distant Garlic relative is an herb that can be used as a Garlic replacement, although the flavor is not as strong or distinctive. It may also be used as a substitute for Garlic chives to decorate and flavor soups and meat dishes. Society Garlic is easy to divide at the bulb and easy to grow; because it is such an easy care plant, many teachers and parents have started to use it for children's or beginner's gardens.

 TULIPA

Also called: *Tulip*

While most American gardeners think that Tulips are native to the Netherlands, they are actually native to Southern Europe, Northern Africa and parts of the Middle East.

Tulips are cultivated worldwide, but their cultivation is most closely associated with the Netherlands in Northern Europe. The cultivation of Tulips in the Netherlands is so traditional that it has become a part of the culture. They are the worlds' largest producer of Tulip bulbs for foreign export.

In America, Tulips are grown as perennial garden flowers. They come in an endless array of colors and variations. Tulips blossom in the spring and last until the early part of summer in North Georgia.

$\mathcal{U}$LMUS CHINENSIS

Also called: Elm or Chinese Elm

The Chinese Elm is a wonderful garden or landscape tree in Atlanta. The Elm's medium size makes it perfect for the urban garden. This tree provides light shade over the garden with its long arching branches. The Elm is deciduous, but its small leaves make for minimal fall cleanup. In the winter, the bare branch structure displays fascinating exfoliating bark and coloration patterns. Tiny orange lenticels can be seen dotting the entire trunk, giving this Chinese native one of its most distinguishing features. Although a relative, this Elm is not the infamous Dutch Elm and thus is not subject to the often-fatal Dutch Elm disease.

In British folklore, the Elm was a home for witches of the forest. The witches used the Elm limbs to make their broom handles and the seeds as a cooking ingredient. Therefore the Elm has been considered sacred to many Wiccan groups throughout the centuries. Elm wood is also known for its use in coffin making, due to its resistance to splitting.

VERONICA

Also called: *Speedwell*

The New England lawyer and poet
Isaac Bassett Choate (1833-1917)
wrote of the Speedwells in his poem
"Speed Well!"

Fair flowers, modest, shy,
In depths of billowy meadow grasses hiding,
And yet worn footpaths nigh
Is found the wonted place of your abiding,
To watch with careless gaze the passer-by!
Your eyes, wide open, tell
In tones of Saxon blue your heart's warm feeling,
As from the hermit's cell
Shines midnight lamp his piety revealing,
The fragrant breath of flowers bids me 'Speed Well!'

An ancient legend from the Roman Catholic Church tells the story of Jesus on his way to the Calvary: "On his way he passed the home of a certain Jewish maiden who, when she saw the drops of agony on his brow, ran after him along the road to wipe his face with her kerchief. This linen, the monks would declare, ever after bore the impress of the sacred features -vera icoma, the 'true likeness.' When the church wished to canonize the pitying maiden, an abbreviated form of the Latin words were given to her, St. Veronica, and her kerchief became one of the most precious relics at St. Peter's where it is said to still be preserved. Medieval flower lovers, whose piety seems to have been eclipsed only by their imaginations, named this little flower from a fancied resemblance to the relic."

VIBURNUM

The Viburnum family is one of the largest plant families in the world. There are many different types of Viburnums, but they do have some characteristics in common. All Viburnums have white flowers and opposite leaf arrangement, meaning the leaves emerge directly across from each other in pairs along the length of the stem. Also, all plants are categorized by how they reproduce; so all Viburnums have a similar flowering and fruiting method. The fruit is a round or oval drupe, red, blue, or black and contains a single seed. Most Viburnum fruits are mildly toxic to humans, but are a great source of food for a wide range of wildlife species.

Viburnums can be deciduous or evergreen, small or large shrubs, or even tree form. Most Viburnums are native to Europe and North America. Tough and durable, there is a Viburnum variety for almost any garden or landscape need. They can be used for screening or for accenting, for their white spring flowers or their cornucopia of fall colors.

Historically, Viburnums have been used for their strong, yet workable wood. The long straight branches of the Viburnum were used to make the arrows found with the mummified remains of Ötzi the Iceman. Ötzi the Iceman and the artifacts found with him, date to 3300 B.C.E.

VISCUM ALBUM

Also called: *Mistletoe*

There was a common belief during the dark ages that Mistletoe did not grow from seeds, but from the souls of the birds that landed in the trees.

Mistletoe was sacred to many peoples and received its greatest veneration from the ancient Celtic and Teutonic tribes of Northern Europe. The Druid priests as part of a sacred ritual gave Mistletoe branches to their worshippers. These branches were taken home and hung from rafters and over doorways to ward off evil spirits.

Later, as these pagan rituals evolved into early Christian tradition, the symbolism of Mistletoe evolved as well. It was first banned in churches as Pagan, only to be accepted later on as its connotation became that of love. As the Christian tradition emerged, Mistletoe's pagan past was all but forgotten. It has now become fully synonymous with Christmas cheer and can be seen displayed over doorways each year at Christmas gatherings across Europe and America.

Mistletoe can easily be recognized by its ball shape and small white berries held in loose clusters between nearly evergreen foliage. It is sometimes hard to see in the summer, but, as autumn brings cooler weather and trees begin to shed their leaves, Mistletoe balls can be seen growing high up in the branches of the larger forest trees.

WISTERIA CHINENSIS

Also called: *Wisteria*

Because Wisteria is one of the most invasive and aggressive scandent vines that grow in the North Georgia area, it is loved or loathed by gardeners all over Atlanta. Once established in a given area, it is nearly impossible to get rid of, second only to Kudzu. Wisteria can be cut off at the ground and will grow right back from the roots. Chemical herbicides do little to curb its growth and it can quickly take over an area as small as a car or as large as a field. If one of the Wisteria leaders touches the ground, it will take root and start a whole new plant. Gardeners need to take care when planting Wisteria and to consider the continual maintenance it will require.

Wisteria can be a beautiful ornamental vine with large purple or white flower racemes that is unmistakable in mid spring. With a sturdy trellis and adroit pruning, a Wisteria may be trained into a tree form. Once the trunk has developed, the trellis can be removed and the Wisteria will be free standing. Wisterias do take several years to begin to produce flowers.

In Japan, Wisteria gardens are grown for public display. One plant, in a flower park, is so large that visitors form lines to walk under its flowers that are cascading down from above. Most varieties are native to Japan and China, although there are several types native to the eastern United States.

ZANTEDESCHIA

Also called: *Calla Lily*

Calla Lilies are a distinctive looking annual or perennial in the Atlanta garden. While they can be planted in the ground, Calla Lilies are most often used in planters and in partner with other flowering plants. They come in colors ranging from white and yellow to pink. Callas are a favorite of florists for their graceful curves that give a unique shape and structure to many floral arrangements.

While Zantedechias are native to South Africa, most American gardeners are familiar with them as a motif in Mexican artwork, most notably the work of Diego Rivera. The genus was named for Italian botanist Giovanni Zantedeschi, who lived from 1773 to 1846. Zantedeschi published several volumes on the flora of Northern Italy.

 Zelkova Serrata

Also called: *Zelkova or Japanese Zelkova*

A strongly vase shaped deciduous tree, the Zelkova is a nearly perfect shade tree for the urban or suburban lawn. The Zelkovas small root structure compared to its canopy makes it a natural choice for the landscape. The mature height of fifty to sixty feet can shade almost any house.

The Zelkova, an Elm relative, is highly resistant to disease and is easy to maintain. The second name Serrata comes from the leaf margin shape, known as serrate. Its leaf structure is also noteworthy for being falcate, curved or scythe shaped.

The Zelkova tree is also a popular choice among Bonsai enthusiasts. Bonsai is a traditional Japanese tree art form.

ℐNDEX OF COMMON PLANT NAMES